The Complete Book of
SPORTS MEDICINE

The Complete Book of SPORTS MEDICINE

An Orthopedist Tells How to Prevent, Evaluate, and Treat Common Injuries

Richard H. Dominguez, M.D.

Illustrations by Julia Bancroft and Timothy Botts

WARNER BOOKS

A Warner Communications Company

Warner Books Edition

Copyright © 1979 Richard H. Dominguez

Warner Books, Inc., 75 Rockefeller Plaza, New York, N.Y. 10019

Printed in the United States of America

First printing: October 1980

10 9 8 7 6 5 4 3 2

Cover design by Gene Light

Cover photo by Bill Cadge

Library of Congress Cataloging in Publication Data

Dominguez, Richard H.
   The complete book of sports medicine.

   Reprint of the 1979 ed. published by Charles Scribner's Sons
597 Fifth Avenue, New York,
N.Y. 10017

   Includes index.
   1. Sports—Accidents and injuries. 2. Sports
medicine. I. Title.
[RD97.D65 1980]   617'.1027   80-15817
ISBN 0-446-37370-2

W A Warner Communications Company

Judy, my wife and best friend, helped and encouraged me in collecting data for my first paper on sports medicine. She also taught me how much fun it is to watch amateur sporting events and has continued to educate me regarding sexism and women in sports.

Dr. George Moreland, Professor Emeritus at Houghton College in Houghton, New York, is the man most responsible for guiding me to the University of Chicago Medical School. He is a dedicated teacher and scholar, whom I have never thanked enough.

To them I dedicate this book.

Contents

1 / Introduction

IF YOU or a member of your family participates in a sport, or in almost any type of physical activity, you have probably asked some of the following questions yourself or made similar statements.

"Do I need to see a doctor for this injury?"

"Should we go to the emergency room now, or can we wait until tomorrow?"

"If only there were some way to read about this problem, doctor, I wouldn't have bothered coming to your office."

"If only I hadn't ignored this! I didn't realize it was that serious!"

"Is this sport safe?"

"Should I get a second opinion?"

"The coach says not to worry. It's minor!"

"I heard the guys talking about carbohydrate loading, and I was wondering . . ."

These problems have become so common because we are in the middle of a sports explosion, and all of us will probably become casualties at one time or another. My office is often filled with individuals whose aches and pains are the result of skiing, running, hitting a ball, or some other sporting endeavor. Many of these people need my attention, others don't, and some could have prevented their injuries, or at least kept them from becoming worse, had they known what to do.

Therefore, I have written this book to provide the kind of medical information needed by people of any age who are already involved or want to become active in a sport or exercise program. First, I have covered the broad medical aspects of sports—the best training methods and the potential danger of others, how to attain fitness and improve performance, and the effects of different drugs on athletics.

I also consider the problems of children and sports, because a proper start in any activity can have a lifelong effect on the individual. Then, for further guidance, I have rated the common sporting activities according to their medical and physiological values, injury risks, and monetary cost.

Finally, I discuss the common sports injuries, starting at the toes and progressing up to the head and out to the fingertips. I explain how to evaluate the severity of an injury, how to treat it, and when to seek emergency care. In addition, I usually discuss recovery time and the amount of disability that can be expected from an injury.

I have attempted at all times to provide sound, tested, and conservative medical advice, with an emphasis on prevention. If used properly, this book should more than pay for itself by saving you worry, disability, and medical expense. It should also make your sport more enjoyable.

Since this guide to sports medicine is for general use, I should also explain that by this term I mean any facet of medicine or science that deals directly or indirectly with a sporting activity.

At a recent meeting of experts on the subject, a panel tried to define sports medicine and its practitioners, but no consensus could be reached. Thus, it is fair to say, that those who practice sports medicine include orthopedic surgeons, family practitioners, pediatricians, internists, physical therapists, athletic trainers, exerciser physiologists, physiologists, psychologists, doctors in biomechanics, engineers, cardiologists, psychiatrists, podiatrists, gynecologists, and others . . . as the list continues to grow. Sports medicine now involves more than the care and prevention of injuries to athletes, it also has to do with the training, fitness, and performance of an individual.

Actually, there is a fundamental difference in the practice of sports medicine in North America and many European countries. In the United States, the first person we see running to an injured football player is a physician. And indeed, historically, the first group of physicians to enter sports medicine in a significant way in this country were orthopedic surgeons.

In Europe a practitioner of sports medicine is usually a physician who is primarily in charge of overseeing the diet, training, and routine testing of an athlete, while the coach handles technique and strategy. Injuries that occur in sports are frequently treated by someone else — a traumatologist or, in some countries, an orthopedic surgeon. In fact, it is not unusual for the physician to be held more responsible than the coach for a poor performance. To see such a shift of responsibility from a coach in this country would be nothing short of revolutionary!

Part One

Sports, Fitness, and Health

2 / Attaining Fitness

A FITNESS craze is sweeping the country. As a result, jogging has become so popular it is now facing a backlash; more and more people are hoping to get in shape by other means, which is certainly possible.

My goal is to simplify the method of attaining fitness, whatever the means. It is not necessary to digest mountains of literature on the subject in order to become fit. Most people can do it very easily, with a little work. The most common problem to overcome is being out of shape.

Why become fit? Because fitness makes life more productive and enjoyable. You will become trimmer, feel and sleep better, be more creative and energetic, and probably live longer. Besides, keeping fit can get to be fun. That is why ten million Americans have taken up jogging to increase their fitness.

By fitness I mean aerobic capacity: the ability of the body to take in large amounts of oxygen through the lungs and pump it through the heart and circulation system to the muscles, where it is used for energy. By my definition, the measurement of one's aerobic capacity is a measurement of one's fitness.

Those who are completely out of shape and have not been playing a sport or exercising regularly should observe the following advice before starting:

1 / Have a medical examination and obtain clearance from a physician if you are over thirty. Many people may fail to do this, even though is the sound way to begin. But it is better to begin exercising without medical confirmation than to postpone both the exercise and the doctor's appointment.

Anyone over thirty who starts an exercise program without seeing a doctor first runs a slight risk of heart attack. If you are over thirty it is best to start with a light exercise program, no matter what kind of shape you are in. If you begin to notice left-sided chest pain, especially if it radiates to your left shoulder or arm, or your left arm goes numb, it is mandatory to stop exercising and seek medical attention at once. These are the classic signs of angina pectoris, the heart pains that represent the body's early warning system. Remember, you have now been told that continued exercise may lead to a heart attack and possibly death.

Other signs that may indicate heart or lung trouble are chest pain in the middle or left side; a deep, burning, chest pain; pain in both shoulders or arms; or wheezing, nausea, or light-headedness. At the first sign of any of these symptoms stop activity and make an appointment to see a physician. Not to do so is foolish at best, suicide at worst.

2 / Follow a weekly schedule of aerobic conditioning—that is, vigorous walking, swimming, jogging, or cycling. Start slowly, with fifteen minutes of exercise every other day. When that stage becomes completely comfortable, add five minutes more. Gradually build strength until thirty minutes of exercise three or four times a week is comfortable. For the average person this should take a month to six weeks to do. If desired, the exercise can be made more strenuous by stepping up the pace, but essentially a person who performs this amount of exercise every week can maintain excellent lifelong fitness doing nothing else. For those interested in meticulously building up an aerobic program, Kenneth Cooper's book *New Aerobics* is full of excellent charts and exercise schedules.

3 / Five minutes after you have stopped exercising, take your pulse at your throat (the easiest and most accurate place for most people to feel it). Count the beats for six seconds and multiply the result by ten. Or for greater accuracy, count them for fifteen seconds and multiply by four. Your pulse should be below 100 counts a minute. If it is higher, your workout was too strenuous —you went too fast or did too much, probably the former. If the pulse is irregular or your heart is skipping beats, you should have gone to the doctor in the first place. Be sure to go now and mention your pulse rate.

In order of preference, I believe the easiest and most readily available forms of exercise are (1) jogging, (2) swimming, and (3) cycling.

Jogging

The first thing to understand about jogging is that it is different from running. Unfortunately, so much has been written about the latter, that by association jogging may now seem more complicated than it actually is. Unlike a number of other authorities on the subject, I think it is pure nonsense for someone who is totally out of shape to do fifteen to twenty minutes of stretching exercises before starting to jog. Jogging is basically a warm-up exercise for many sports. To begin, just do it! All that is required is proper shoes, suitable clothing, and attainable goals.

A good pair of training flats is mandatory. Trying to cut costs by running in a worn-out pair of gym shoes or indeed any type of ordinary gym shoes will lead to trouble in the form of at least frustration if not painful foot or leg problems. The best guide to shoes is the one that appears every autumn in *Runner's World*. It lists the twenty best training and racing shoes and rates them by quality, cost, and suitability according to body build, distances, and surfaces. An alternate suggestion is to ask the salesman in a good athletic-shoe store how the various shoes have been rated and what he recommends. Any shoe salesman worth his salt will be familiar with that guide, since millions of dollars are made or lost each year as a result of how running shoes are rated. Select the shoe that best suits your needs, independent of cost considerations. The cheapest one may be just right for you.

Wear loose clothing. Fancy, expensive jogging outfits are unnecessary, but comfortable shorts and a shirt, both made of smooth materials that breathe well, will do in almost any temperate to warm climate. Avoid scratchy or ridged materials that could become very irritating to the chest or crotch over prolonged periods of exercise.

Now for goals. A reasonable amount of jogging for a beginner is fifteen to thirty minutes three or four times a week (about once every other day). If you are totally out of condition it is better to give your body a day between workouts to avoid the common problems and overuse syndromes that many adults develop from pushing themselves too hard. Here's where I very strongly recommend Dr. Cooper's charts to my patients.

As a general rule, start jogging very, very slowly, at a pace you can comfortably maintain. Run with the heel first or the foot flat; do not get up on the ball of the foot so that it hits the ground first—this is a sprinting or fast running technique, not a jogging or distance-running position. I think it is sprinting that defeats so many people. They start out thinking that they need to run as fast as they can, so they begin on the balls of their feet and are totally exhausted in one or two minutes.

The most efficient way to get into shape is to perform an activity continuously. Walking or jogging without stopping is far better than sprinting and having to stop and recover from the exertion. Jogging is done at a very slow, steady pace, not much faster than a fast walk. In fact, a brisk walk is close to jogging, and can be substituted for it, if you prefer.

Any foot or leg pain that develops while running should bring a halt to the exercise. To proceed in spite of pain may lead to the development of an overuse syndrome, or to a chronic, painful disability. A sensible beginning with judicious rest when necessary will amply reward you in terms of better health.

A last word of advice about jogging concerns the jogging surface. Generally, the softer the surface, the less shock there is to the feet and legs. In order of decreasing hardness, these are the most common surfaces available: concrete, asphalt, dirt, artificial turf, bark, and sand. If you have a choice, bark is ideal because it is so easy on the legs, and it is not too soft. Sand can be too yielding and taxing.

As with any exercise, keep in mind that it takes time to build up endurance. It is not only the heart and lungs that need toughening, but the tissue, ligaments, and bones in your feet and legs as well. There is no way to rush it, so don't overdo.

Swimming

Swimming is the second sport I recommend for conditioning. It is close to an ideal activity, since it exercises all the muscles and removes some of the strains of gravity on the body. For most people the exercise value of swimming is almost as good as that of jogging. Ironically, the worse a swimmer is, the better exercise it becomes.

Excellent swimming lessons for children are available at the YMCA. For adults who already know how to swim, I strongly recommend participation in a Masters group at a local YMCA or American Athletic Union club. Almost all YMCAs have a Masters swim program that provides good advice on stroke mechanics in an informal way. In addition, Masters groups usually swim at a convenient time for people who work, and they set aside a lane for slow swimmers so no one needs to feel uncomfortable about a lack of proficiency. There are also Masters' swim meets, if you are so inclined.

Cycling

Cycling is the next best exercise to swimming for fitness, and there are two ways to do it. The classic one is cycling outdoors, which is also a good means of transportation. For those who are really serious about cycling and need a new bicycle, I recommend reading *Consumer Reports.* The magazine compares the cost, durability, and dependability of ten-speed bicycles, as well as the comfort of various seats. (Obviously, a ten-speed bike is not necessary if you have another model at hand.) The seat and reliability of the bicycle are important factors that affect one's enjoyment of the sport. To avoid the chafing, discomfort, and skin problems that can occur when cycling, a pair of cycling shorts is advisable. These are available at any good bicycle shop.

For people who are not interested in cycling outside, or find that the climate is not conducive to the activity year-round, an exercise bike set up indoors will do very nicely. Prices of these machines range from under $100 to $500, depending on the sophistication and calibration of the bicycle. Again, the *Consumer Reports* evaluations are very good, if you intend to invest in such a device.

If boredom is a problem while cycling indoors, then place the bicycle near a radio or television set for distraction.

Arthritis

Most people with arthritis are able to exercise in a swimming pool, but it should only be done under the guidance of a physician. This is especially true in cases of rheumatoid arthritis, which can affect the heart and lungs. If the arthritis involves only the hips, knees, or ankles and not the upper extremities, cycling might be possible, as long as it doesn't irritate the joints. If there is any arthritis in the upper extremities, the pressure from leaning on the handlebars of a bicycle might be a problem and prevent cycling. In my opinion, an arthritic joint will not benefit from the repetitive pounding of jogging or running, so I cannot recommend those forms of exercise to anyone with an arthritic joint in a lower extremity.

Asthma

Asthma should not stop an athlete. Wheezing and shortness of breath or an asthmatic attack that occurs during or after vigorous activity is known medically as exercise-induced asthma, often referred to as EIA. Occasionally the initials EIB are used to indicate exercise-induced bronchospasm, but, for practical purposes, these conditions are the same.

No one really knows what causes EIA or why some activities tend to promote it more than others, but here are a few facts you should know:

1 / Ninety percent of all people who have asthma will develop EIA if they exercise hard enough.

2 / Approximately forty percent of all people who are allergic to substances like pollen will develop EIA as well.

3 / EIA can usually be treated and prevented quite successfully with proper medical care and counseling.

4 / The worst sport or sporting activity for people with a tendency to develop EIA is free, vigorous, prolonged running.

5 / The sport least likely to cause EIA is swimming. Many physicians feel that swimming is good medical treatment for EIA. An Olympic season has not passed in recent years without at least one asthma-afflicted athlete winning a gold medal in this sport.

6 / Bicycling, as it affects those prone to EIA, is somewhere between swimming and free running.

7 / Kayaking, rowing, and crew cause minimal EIA.

Doctors do not understand why swimming and kayaking cause minimal asthmatic attacks, while running causes great problems. Most likely it is not the physical movements involved but humidity that makes the big difference.

While prolonged running is the worst activity for EIA, running for short spurts of less than two to three minutes is not usually a problem. However, if long distance running is the sport of preference, remember that Jim Ryan is an asthmatic—and he succeeded in spite of this difficulty. Some long distance runners have found that they can "run through the asthma." Before attempting this, however, the individual should be under proper medical care.

No amount of training or specific medication will guarantee the prevention of an asthmatic attack; training in swimming may help, but not with certainty. Many studies have shown that no amount of training or conditioning will affect the sensitivity of the lungs.

Thus, the first and best recommendation for an asthmatic person is to choose a sport wisely. A second suggestion is to discuss some of the various medications with a doctor. A safe and often effective medicine is sodium cromolyn in aerosol form, if it can be tolerated. This medication is only available by prescription.

Another suggestion is to avoid conditions that aggravate asthma and make it more difficult to control. These include cold, smog and other forms of air pollution, wind, fog, emotional stress, and infection. The season of the year may also have a lot to do with asthmatic attacks. Certain athletes find that they will have much more discomfort in the spring or fall, depending on their specific allergies.

A last suggestion is to keep track of any specific location where wheezing occurs. Some athletes have found that a specific type of grass, such as rye grass, will give them trouble, whereas playing on artificial surfaces or other types of grass causes no difficulty. In fact, even swimming cannot guarantee immunity from certain conditions—the varying levels of chlorine content in water can also make a significant difference to someone with EIA.

In the past, an asthmatic child was often removed from physical education classes by the coach, his parents, or even a physician. This often resulted in an unfortunate situation for the child, who began to feel inferior. Such problems can easily be avoided by proper understanding. The parent, child, coach, physical educator, and physician should all work together.

Bad Back

Back problems benefit most from swimming because it exercises all the correct muscles for spinal support while removing the stress of body weight from the back. In most cases, jogging is also good for bad backs, but stop if it aggravates the pain. The same is true of cycling. Always listen to your body's signals as soon as you receive them; it is foolish to do otherwise.

Diabetes

Most people with diabetes are aware of how to manage their problem in regard to exercise programs. However, it is absolutely senseless to begin such a program without the consent of a physician and without monitoring the diabetes. Almost any type of exercise can be performed if it is properly supervised.

Fever

Exercise of any type is unsafe with a fever because one type of virus is known to mimic a cold, the flu, or even mononucleosis, and, at times, it can also affect the heart. If this virus is present, exercising in the face of a fever risks damage to the heart. This is true for people of any age from 10 to 100. After recovery is sure and the temperature is back to normal, an exercise program can be resumed gradually, but never, ever, exercise or participate in sports when feverish.

Hypertension, or High Blood Pressure

People with high blood pressure should not begin an exercise program before discussing it with a physician, especially if any medication is involved. A case of essential hypertension (hypertension that develops without any apparent cause) may very well benefit from exercises, but they must be done under medical guidance.

Lung Problems

Many people who are disabled by such lung conditions as emphysema and chronic bronchitis will benefit from a controlled exercise program. Carefully monitored swimming exercises are best. They are excellent for the lungs and improve overall fitness. Unfortunately, not many of these programs are generally available.

Medications

Anyone on any medication whatsoever would be unwise to begin an exercise program before consultation with a physician. Many medicines behave differently during exercise and may also affect the body's ability to react to the stress of exercise.

Obesity

Anyone more than thirty-five pounds overweight should have a physical examination and receive dietary advice from a physician before starting to exercise in earnest. An aerobic exercise program will definitely increase the ability to lose weight. Such a program will "burn off" fat, and it will also decrease cravings for carbohydrates and high-calorie foods, thereby helping to maximize weight loss. Brisk walking, jogging, cycling, and swimming are the best activities to start with. Swimming may be the easiest, because the buoyancy of water removes the stresses of weight during exercise. Many people with very heavy thighs may find chafing a significant problem during exercise. Clothing made of a synthetic fabric similar in texture to silk may eliminate the irritation. Vaseline will also decrease chafing and make such activities as jogging more tolerable.

Old Injuries

People with old knee injuries, or "bad" knees, hips, or ankles will find it very difficult, if not impossible, to take up jogging. I recommend jogging only when it is comfortable and does not bother a painful joint. If pain or swelling develops in a knee or ankle, you may be forced to turn to another sport like swimming for aerobic training. Since the effects of gravity are removed in the water, swimming does not make the same demands as jogging on the lower extremities. In fact, it is much easier to achieve fitness in the water than on land.

If swimming has no appeal, substitute cycling. Many knee and ankle problems are not aggravated by this activity, so if it is comfortable and enjoyable, by all means take it up. People with hip problems also find that cycling is a splendid way to strengthen the appropriate muscles around the hip and to exercise the hip joint without harming it.

Post-heart-attack Patients

There no longer seems to be much question about the effectiveness of rehabilitating heart-attack victims through a carefully controlled exercise program. There are only two problems involved: many patients must overcome their fear of entering such a program; and, after starting, many aggressive people push themselves too hard when exercising. This is why it is mandatory to have an exercise program outlined by a physician. Ideally, the exercises should be set up as part of a cardiac rehabilitation program affiliated with a hospital. Such programs are very carefully monitored with EKGs, which use telemetry to check a patient's cardiogram while he or she exercises on a calibrated bicycle or treadmill. Again, after a heart attack it is extremely unwise and unsafe to begin an exercise program without expert guidance.

3 / Training

ALL MEN and women are not created physically equal. Among individuals of both sexes there are great variations in height, muscle composition, ligament flexibility, and that vague something called coordination. An occasional champion possesses the right combination of all of these variables, but the fact that there are so many variables gives all of us certain abilities that fit us better for some sports than for others. The following discussion concerns the ways in which strength, speed, and endurance are developed through appropriate muscle training.

Aerobic and Anaerobic Energy Formation

One type of energy formation is aerobic, which literally means "with air or oxygen." Aerobic capacity is the ability of a person to breathe in large amounts of air and circulate it through the lungs and heart into the body and throughout the entire muscle system for energy formation. To be in truly good condition, an individual must have good aerobic capacity.

Aerobic activities require at least two minutes of continuous activity, and this type of training is the best for overall physical fitness, since it builds up endurance of the heart and lungs. Jogging, running, swimming and cycling are the most common forms of aerobic training, but the best of all is cross-country skiing. Typical aerobic sporting events include cross-country, running, and skiing, but soccer and basketball also make great aerobic demands.

Any activity that lasts less than two minutes depends on anaerobic (without air) metabolism. The energy for anaerobic metabolism is stored in the muscles in the form of glycogen (a carbohydrate) for instant use, but it won't last for more than two minutes. In anaerobic training, the muscles that react most to strenuous activity are conditioned to tolerate lactic acid, a by-product of the conversion of glycogen to energy. This type of training may also increase the enzymes that process glycogen and it may help to develop fast-reacting or fast-twitch, muscles. The general fatigue, combined with pain or discomfort that most of us feel after hard exercise is a result of lactic-acid build-up in the muscle system. Typical anaerobic sporting events are the 100-yard or -meter dash, swimming races, and short runs in baseball or football, sports in which bursts of energy are followed by long periods of inactivity.

The special resources required by anaerobic events are developed through interval training, which involves short periods of strenuous exertion interspersed with periods of rest. Wind sprints are a common form of such training. These consist of running at near top speed for a distance of 40 to 100 yards, stopping for a varying time, and then repeating the sequence, as necessary. If anaerobic training is continued and the rest intervals are short enough, an aerobic training effect can also be acquired. In other words, both aerobic function and speed can be increased with this training. To receive a training effect, it is always best to practice at about 90 percent of performance speed. Very little effect is derived at speeds below 75 to 80 percent of performance level. In practical terms, this means a sprinter has to practice at almost full speed to see any improvement at all. Anyone who "dogs it" in practice will show no increase in speed, even though he or she goes through all the motions. Of course adolescents who are still growing but practice poorly will continue to improve, because normal growth increases their strength and size. But good anaerobic training will produce an even greater improvement in their performance.

All of this points to the fact that training must be specific to the event in which an athlete expects to participate. In a sense, anaerobic training is the most difficult, and it proves the old coaching adage that "we perform the way we practice."

Understanding the difference between aerobic and anaerobic events makes clear why many football and baseball players (and even some sprinters) can get away with being out of condition and still perform well. Their overall condition or aerobic capacity is not taxed by the short duration of their activity. They are able to get by with the

God-given amount of high energy stored in their muscles. But they would be better off if they trained aerobically as well as anaerobically.

Most gifted athletes in anaerobic events are able to get away with little training until they pass the state level of competition. Some truly gifted people are even able to get away with it on the national level, but on the international Olympic scene there are virtually no athletes who are able to succeed without a significant degree of aerobic training.

Stressing the need for aerobic training is not meant to de-emphasize the value of anaerobic training. Clearly, there is a need for both types. A classic example of mistraining is seen in swimming. For years, swimming coaches have used aerobic training methods—that is, long, slow, endurance training—for what is essentially an anaerobic sport: most swimming events are over in less than two minutes. Now, weight training and the trend toward more anaerobic or interval training techniques are both helping to improve swimming performances.

Muscle Composition

Basic muscle makeup varies greatly between individuals. The differences are primarily attributed to two common types of muscle fiber: slow-twitch and fast-twitch. Slow-twitch fibers are considered endurance fibers and are especially helpful in aerobic activities, while the fast-twitch fibers are essential for anaerobic or sprinting events.

It is thought that those people who have a high number of slow-twitch fibers are natural endurance runners and those with a high percentage of fast-twitch fibers are natural sprinters. However, recent evidence indicates that training can change the ratio of those fibers. So the old adage "Speed is a gift, endurance is an accomplishment" is no longer true. A more appropriate saying would be: "Both speed and the ability to endure are gifts, and both can be improved with training."

The difference in muscle composition explains why some people have a great deal of difficulty getting into jogging endurance programs. They probably have a high proportion of fast-twitch fibers, which build up lactic acid in the blood more rapidly than slow-twitch fibers. This results in muscle pain and a feeling of fatigue. On the other hand, these fast-twitch muscle people are gifted with the ability to sprint, and frequently find that they need little training for anaerobic sporting events. They are the so-called drop dead sprinters who are good for one short sprint which exhausts them. Such people would benefit and improve with aerobic training, but they usually don't feel the need for it until they are beyond the high school or state level of competition.

A similar problem occurs to some people who have done only extensive aerobic conditioning. When participating in touch football, a swimming contest, or a sprint at a picnic, they find themselves as tired as everybody else, much to their chagrin. However, they probably recovered faster than the winners who actually were out of condition. One solution to this problem is to do some kind of interval training that will provide both anaerobic and aerobic conditioning.

Tapering

Certain sports that require a great deal of training also require a period of relative rest prior to peak performance. This enforced rest period is called tapering. The art of coaching includes the ability to put the proper amount of stress on athletes so they benefit from training and then, at the right time, to taper their training so they will achieve maximum performance during the big event. Tapering is an art, but, in my opinion, it can only be done three or at most four times a year to get the right results. Most coaches will taper their players only twice a year.

If tapering fails to make an improvement in an athlete's results, the individual may have overtrained. When this happens, the body becomes fatigued and rundown and the person requires more rest than normal to achieve top performance. In this regard, I see absolutely no reason for seven-day-a-week training or practice schedules. I know that some coaches still hold to the belief that a day lost from training is a day lost forever, but the merits of that idea have not been scientifically proved and experience tends to show otherwise. Even on a world-class level, I know of no evidence to support any damage resulting from one day of rest a week. On the contrary, rest is of great psychological benefit to an athlete, and, since the quality of training is much more important than the quantity, the mental aspect is more important than most of us realize.

Actually, for individuals under the age of ten, four days of training a week is probably the most I would recommend. We all need time off, and children need more than adults. They spend a lot of energy just in growing, and this should be taken into consideration when making physical demands on them. Even during the high school years, allowance should be made for this form of energy expenditure.

Weight Training

There are three types of weight training: isotonic, isometric, and isokinetic. In a truly competitive sport, with the possible exception of running, the athlete who does weight training will do better than the one who doesn't and will probably have less joint, tendon, and ligament problems.

Isotonic, or Olympic, weight lifting consists of lifting barbells and is sometimes called "pumping iron." Strength and body-building can be achieved with isotonic weight lifting, and it is the most popular form of such exercise because it is so readily available and so easy to measure. Barbells can be fashioned inexpensively, and reasonably-priced weight sets are sold in almost every sporting goods store.

The problem with isotonic weightlifting is that it may not provide all the benefits a person is looking for. Because of the configuration of the muscles and joints in such areas as the elbow or knee, muscles get more exercise in some places than in others. In other words, the amount of muscle exercise required to move a joint may vary considerably. Thus, pure muscle strength may be increased, but the ability to perform a certain task may not be equally improved. For example, being able to lift a hundred pounds more with your legs does not necessarily increase your running speed.

Isometric exercises strengthen the muscles and joints by flexing the muscles; no other movement is required. Some classic isometric exercises consist of pulling on a fixed bar or pushing against a wall. Although the joints are not moved during these exercises, they can be strengthened as much as desired in this fashion. For certain injured joints and other rehabilitations, this form of exercise is often much safer than any other. It will even permit the strengthening of a limb in a cast. Another advantage of isometrics is that they require no special equipment. They are done simply by tightening the muscles in an area, holding them as tight as possible for five to ten seconds, relaxing, and then repeating the exercise over and over again. Thus, isometrics provide a very good, safe, inexpensive, and effective way to strengthen a muscle or muscles and stay in shape.

The current "in" way to strengthen muscles is through isokinetic exercise, or by moving the muscles against an even pressure. The advantage of isokinetic exercise is that it applies an equal amount of force throughout a joint's entire range of motion (as opposed to the unequal stress a barbell would exert on the same area). In fact, the extensive research that has been done on strengthening in general seems to indicate that isokinetic exercise is the best way to strengthen muscles for almost any activity.

Isokinetic strengthening requires sophisticated exercise machines, however. The least expensive models of this type are the so-called mini-gyms. Basically, these units consist of a bar on the end of a very strong cable or rope that is attached to a small machine. The faster one pulls, lifts, or jumps against the bar, the more resistance is encountered. But, unlike weight lifting, there is no way to gauge numerically how well you are doing since most of these machines are not calibrated. You can't walk away from one and boast of lifting two hundred pounds, for example. Any benefit derived from such a machine is directly related to the effort a person puts into the exercises. That is why it is so easy to slack off and not give it your best effort. The only truly calibrated isokinetic exercise machine available is the Cybex, but it is very expensive, so there are few organizations (other than wealthy professional teams and research labs) that can afford to own one.

Another well known exercise machine is the Nautilus, a kind of hybrid between the isokinetic and isotonic systems of exercise that offers weights as well as a sophisticated system of pulley and lever actions. A Nautilus is excellent for strengthening a specific muscle, such as the biceps or quadriceps. But isokinetic machines are better at strengthening a specific function, such as jumping. Proponents of both the Nautilus and isokinetic systems are very vocal, of course, but neither side has yet had the final say.

Women, as well as men, should lift weights, although they do not develop the same bulging muscles of the male physique. This is probably due to female hormones, or the lack of male hormones.

Weight Lifting for Children and Adolescents

Virtually nothing has been published about the virtues or disadvantages of weight lifting and weight training for children, so the following is my opinion, based on my experience in treating children and their injuries.

Weight lifting for children under ten is total nonsense and probably of no value. Any strengthening that occurs in a child will happen in the course of normal growth and activity, regardless of weight lifting.

For children between the ages of eleven and thirteen, it's difficult to judge. I would not forbid weight lifting, but I would never start a general, formalized weight-lifting program for all children between those ages. If a child is highly motivated and wants to lift weights alone, without supervision, I think it is safe to let him or her fool around with an occasional barbell or isokinetic machine. But I believe more harm than good may result from formalized weight-lifting programs at this stage.

Weight training at the high-school level can be of benefit, however. The approach to most sports has become so scientific that athletes from the ages of fourteen or fifteen up will benefit from some kind of weight-lifting program.

A word of caution must be given in regard to adolescents who begin weight training. A rapidly growing individual who lifts weights may experience a pull-off fracture (see page 56) from overexertion or from losing control of the weights. This is less likely to occur on the isokinetic or Nautilus machines, but it is not impossible.

Flexibility

Flexibility among individuals can vary as dramatically as muscle composition and body size. Someone who is gifted with exceptional flexibility is commonly referred to as being double-jointed.

As a general rule, flexible people gain little from stretching exercises and probably don't need them. But these people feel good after stretching and tend to advocate it. Actually, they would derive more benefit from strengthening exercises.

Because great flexibility is a natural endowment, those who have it frequently have little insight into the problems of those who are tight-jointed, and don't understand how they could be so different. Some people can simply do the splits or sit swami style with ease, while others find such positions impossible.

Flexibility can be increased gradually by gentle stretching exercises and the proper balancing of muscle strength. For example, if the strength of the biceps in the front of the upper arm and that of the triceps in the back of the upper arm are equalized, or balanced, flexibility may be increased. But no matter how many stretching exercises a tight-jointed person may do, some extreme postures will always be impossible.

Massage

In general, massage should be used only for sore muscles or in warming up for sports. To aid in rehabilitation, it should be done under a doctor's direction, because it can aggravate an injury and increase bleeding.

Warm-ups

One of the best warm-ups for any sport is jogging. After five to seven minutes of jogging, when a light sweat develops, one should also do stretching and calisthenics particular to the sport, for another five to seven minutes.

In tennis, the second part of warming up may consist of slow volleying and serving. After suffering an injury, one should not attempt warm-ups until normal strength has returned and 90 percent of normal motion is possible.

Neuromuscular Coordination

Natural athletic abilities may vary, but there is almost nothing in medical literature relating to a definition or measurement of the differences between athletes, and undertaking such studies would be extremely difficult. We could try to measure the ability of nerves to send messages from the brain to the muscles, but this would require very sophisticated equipment as well as much time and expense. It would be equally difficult to study hand-eye coordination and other physical phenomena. For now, we have to be content with saying that such abilities are God-given gifts, but that does not mean they cannot be improved with practice and training.

4 / Diet and Drugs

CERTAINLY no subject causes greater controversy in all of sports than the use of diet and drugs to enhance performance. Therefore, I will try to provide the information necessary for obtaining maximum results. This material is based on hard scientific data, not on hearsay.

Diet

Unfortunately, much of what athletes eat and take into their bodies is influenced by locker-room conversation and the sports grapevine. The positive effect athletes feel or get from a drug or food is usually of psychological origin, what is known as a placebo effect. A physician, coach, or parent who administers any medicine stating "This medicine will make you perform better" is likely to see some improvement. A placebo effect will occur fifty percent of the time even with an ineffective medication. Anything that promises to increase quickness, endurance, or power will often achieve those results simply because the athlete believes in it.

For example, there is no scientific evidence that any vitamin will directly improve performance. Better performance in the form of increased speed, strength, and endurance is the result of proper aerobic and anaerobic training and appropriate weight training. Athletes tend to be tremendous copycats, as are coaches, so if someone performs better, they assume it must be the result of a medication or something other than harder work in training and they rush to try it themselves.

The best diet is also the best-kept secret in all of sports, and, given human nature, is likely to remain so. If this diet is followed, no athlete will need additional vitamins, minerals, or protein additives, and top performance will be obtained at the optimum weight.

This "secret" diet is a well-balanced assortment of standard foods, consisting of approximately 15 percent protein, 35 percent fat, and 50 percent carbohydrate. The essential foods can be divided into four basic groups—dairy products, meat and other proteins, vegetables and fruits, and breads and cereals—plus some additional foods that are supplements, but not really a group in themselves. Any athlete, even when training or performing, can maintain excellent health by following the daily diet given below.

Dairy Products

Foods: Whole milk, skim milk, buttermilk, evaporated or dry milk, American or cheddar cheese, and ice cream.

Daily Servings: At least two for adults, four for teenagers, and three for children.

Meats and Other Proteins

Foods: Beef, veal, lamb, pork, fish, poultry, eggs, and cottage cheese.

Daily Servings: Two or more, of four to five ounces each, cooked except for the cottage cheese.

Vegetables and Fruits

Foods: A dark green or deep yellow vegetable; citrus fruit or juice; other fruits and vegetables, including potatoes. A food from each of these three categories must be part of each day's menu.

Daily Servings: Four or more.

Breads and Cereals

Foods: Wholegrain, enriched, or restored bread or cereal.
Daily Servings: Four or more.

Additional Foods

Normal amounts of butter, oil, margarine, sugar, and sweets can be included to provide additional enjoyment and calories, but these foods do not replace those from the other four groups.

The reason this diet will probably not be followed is that no one takes it seriously. Everyone is convinced that a secret energy food or vitamin must exist. But the critical factors affecting performance are actually the whole diet and a proper balance of foods. Some foods actually slow a person down and make him sluggish, others contain too much fat, and the wrong kind can be harmful.

A classic example is the use of sugars. For years, parents or coaches have given children sugar cubes, dextrose pills, honey, or hard candy for extra energy. All this does is cause excess fluid to be pulled into the athlete's intestines, possibly causing some dehydration. Remember, the energy for many events should already be stored in the muscle for use (see pages 13–14).

At game time, the best food to take is a limited amount of a non-carbonated fruit juice or non-carbonated soft drink. In small amounts these beverages will provide refreshment, and their sugar content is low enough to be harmless. During any event of significant duration, don't restrict water.

For most activities, eat a well-balanced normal meal three hours prior to participation. In the pregame meal it is wise to limit fat and protein, which are digested slowly. This is especially true if the activity is of long duration. Foods that produce gas should also be avoided.

Again, the best way to achieve top performance at the optimum weight is to have a well-balanced diet together with properly planned and executed training. Among equally gifted athletes, the one who eats the most sensibly and trains the best will always outperform the others.

Carbohydrate Loading

Carbohydrate loading is a technique that has been much discussed since Erich Segal did a TV essay on the subject at the 1976 Montreal Olympics. Its main use is in endurance athletic events, such as the marathon.

The method starts with heavy training on a low carbohydrate diet, and then, prior to the main event, switches to light training with a high carbohydrate diet. This procedure can double the amount of glycogen in the body. Glycogen is an energy-giving sugar that is stored in the muscles, so theoretically the amount of energy available is doubled. World-class marathon runners and other competitors who undergo at least two hours of endurance activity probably do gain from this regimen. But they are the *only* ones who can benefit, no matter how active an athlete is.

Unfortunately, when glycogen is stored in a muscle, three times the normal amount of water is also pulled into the muscle. This leads to a definite feeling of sluggishness, heaviness, and stiffness, which can be felt in the heart. As a result of this practice, angina-like heart pains have been reported in athletes, and cardiogram changes have occurred. In addition, extra glycogen can destroy muscle tissue.

In brief, a world-class runner or similar endurance athlete can safely attempt carbohydrate loading, but anyone else takes a big risk trying it. Once again, a well-balanced diet and sensible eating and drinking are the best keys to success.

Weight Gain

Many athletes, especially growing boys, want to increase the size of their bodies. What they really want is weight gain in muscle mass, but too often they associate this with extra food, which will only add fat. Eating meat has no special effect, either. The only way to gain muscle mass is to increase it through appropriate muscle training. The maximum rate of gain is one to two pounds of muscle mass per week, given the right exercises.

The body of an average American middle-class boy is 15 percent fat, but optimal performance weight is only 5 percent body fat. Thus, the average teenage male can afford to lose 10 percent of his body weight without doing himself any harm—if the weight is lost at a rate of no more than two to four pounds a week. Weight loss—as in "making" (losing) weight for boxing and wrestling—in excess of that amount is done at the expense of muscle mass and, therefore, of strength and performance. Any child who is thin or skinny is already below the national average, and no weight loss is warranted.

The use of any medication to achieve weight loss in athletics is condemnable. Catastrophic medical consequences, including hospitalization, intensive medical treatment, and, at times, surgery, have resulted from injudicious amounts of weight loss, especially in thin boys. If a child is so overweight that significant loss is necessary, it should be done under a doctor's care. For preteens trying to "make weight" for a sport, I cannot justify any weight losing routines. Somehow a preteen making weight for a sport doesn't seem to be sport at all.

Vitamins

Some experts in sports medicine have called vitamins "urine-discoloring placebos." That's not exactly true, but here are the facts about them in regard to sports.

Vitamins A and D are unquestionably toxic. When taken in excess, they can even be life threatening. They have no place in athletic training in quantities above the standard recommended daily allowance.

B complex vitamins are adequately provided by a balanced diet. Fortunately, these vitamins are water soluble, so any excess will pass through the body. The only B vitamin that might affect sports activity is nicotinic acid, or niacin. Taken in excess, it can be harmful to cardiac muscle during exercise.

Vitamin E is toxic in animals. It is thought to be toxic in human beings as well, and there is accumulating evidence to suggest that this is indeed so. There is absolutely no evidence that vitamin E improves athletic performance.

Vitamin C. Low doses of vitamin C may very well be beneficial. However, too much vitamin C increases the destruction of vitamin B_{12}, increases the risk of kidney stones, and may cause scurvy, the disease for which it was originally used as a preventative. In fact, high doses of vitamin C may cause an allergic reaction. It is fair to say that an allergy to a life-sustaining vitamin would be potentially life threatening, so there is no place for high doses of vitamin C in athletics.

Now you see why vitamins are not simply "urine-discoloring placebos." They can, in fact, be quite harmful, and I believe megavitamin therapy should be avoided. Given the junk food age in which we live, any one-a-day-type vitamin can be helpful, but anything more than that is wasteful and really not defensible, with the possible exception of vitamin C in a low dosage.

Iron

Approximately 10 to 20 percent of young female athletes may suffer iron depletion. This deficiency is usually the result of iron lost in blood during menstruation combined with iron lost in sweat while training for running or swimming. Swimmers do perspire, but they are usually unaware of it because the water washes the sweat away. If a girl or woman seems overly fatigued, it's reasonable to have a blood count taken. If she is anemic or has a low hemoglobin level, an intake of supplemental iron is warranted, under a physician's guidance. Males should take iron only under a doctor's prescription because they have no way to lose it regularly. Excessive iron intake can be toxic in both sexes, and over a period of years can cause cirrhosis of the liver.

Drugs

Aspirin and Other Pain-relieving Drugs

Aspirin (acetylsalicylic acid) is still the most effective medicine of its kind available. The aspirin substitutes such as acetaminophen may be almost as effective as analgesics (pain relievers) but they lack aspirin's anti-inflammatory properties. Some of the new wonder drugs have many of the effects of aspirin and, in fact, may be safer in some circumstances, but some of them are certainly more toxic. For athletics aspirin is invaluable—if taken properly.

Mild to moderate joint aches, mild tendinitis, mild bruises, and even moderately severe bruises are very nicely treated with aspirin taken in the proper manner. The problem is, many people don't take aspirin seriously. When it is prescribed, they feel that their physician is not taking them seriously enough, and they do not take it as directed. For this reason, many physicians have given up trying to advise it and have instead turned to more expensive drugs that people seem to find more appealing.

Nonetheless, aspirin will improve swollen joints, and it helps to speed up their recovery. It should be taken at regular intervals (every four, six, or eight hours, depending on the dosage) spread out over the day, not on a hit-or-miss basis. Someone weighing between 50 and 100 pounds can safely take a total of four to five aspirin throughout the day, preferably after meals, on a full stomach, or with milk or ice cream. An individual who weighs between 100 and 200 pounds can take eight to ten aspirin throughout the day, and for those over 200 pounds, up to fifteen aspirin a day is a safe dosage.

In addition to the fact that it is not taken seriously, aspirin can be toxic in doses not much greater than those that provide the most effective relief therapeutically. The danger symptoms to look out for when taking aspirin are stomach upset, stomach cramps, or any ulcer-type symptoms. Anyone with ulcers or colitis should never take aspirin. If females notice increased bruising or increased menstrual periods when taking aspirin, they should discontinue its use. Ringing in the ears is also an indication that a person is taking too much of the drug.

As for similar generic medications, the cheapies are usually as effective as brands A, B, and C, even if they do not get into the blood stream as quickly. This should make no difference if the level of aspirin in the blood is maintained throughout the day by taking it at equal intervals.

Some people believe that if they take aspirin when they are young, it will not work as well when they are older. But tolerance levels for aspirin do not develop in the body, nor does aspirin become addictive. Used properly, it is an excellent drug.

Amphetamines

Amphetamines ("uppers," "Speed," Dexedrine) are potent drugs that can give one a feeling of extra energy or alertness. If an individual is fatigued, depressed, sleepy, disinterested, or bored, it is possible he or she will suddenly *feel* like playing or performing after taking an amphetamine.

But amphetamines do not actually improve performance, and they do not improve reaction time. They delude the taker into thinking that he or she is quicker, better, or more alert. In fact, amphetamines almost certainly decrease one's ability to react to a changing situation. A person can more easily be "faked out," confused, or even disoriented after taking a drug of this kind. If taken over an extended period of time, amphetamines will cause weight loss and probably some brain damage, and they will become addictive.

Recently there have been claims that some football players, especially defensive linemen, take uppers in very high doses to improve performance. High doses of amphetamines probably changed the way these players felt and acted, so perhaps they were able to play with a higher pain threshold, but their performance could not have improved and their ability to adapt had to lessen. For this reason, amphetamines may increase the risk of injury.

These potent and potentially dangerous drugs have no place in sports medicine. Besides, vigorous exercise and sports give their own natural "high"; using drugs will only cheat an athlete of that very real pleasure.

Barbiturates

Barbiturates (or "downers") have no place in sports medicine, either. These drugs are very habit forming, and people who take them find they need ever-increasing doses to calm down. Since barbiturates decrease reaction time and performance, I can only think they would be used in sports by unethical individuals attempting to drug an athlete into a poor performance.

Barbiturate withdrawal is the worst kind known in medicine, even worse than heroin withdrawal. When a person who has been taking barbiturates for a period of time quits cold turkey, he or she will frequently have seizures and possibly suffer brain damage, or even die —a not uncommon occurrence in barbiturate withdrawal.

The one exception to the preceding discussion is athletes with seizure disorders. They frequently need to be on these drugs for life, and if properly managed medically, barbiturates should not affect the ability of these people to participate in an activity.

Beer

In general, the effects of beer on exercise have not been well studied scientifically, but its use in most activities is not recommended. It will decrease performance in skill and concentration events; it releases gas in the intestine from its carbonation; and it is high in calories, and so should be avoided by anyone for whom weight is a problem.

Beer may be of benefit to some athletes during long endurance events because it provides both fluids and calories. And alcohol is a potent pain reliever, so it is easy to see why some endurance athletes swear by beer; it helps them endure by deadening the pain.

Caffeine

Caffeine may be the only drug that will truly improve performance. In a recent article Dr. David Costil, a foremost exercise physiologist, claimed that one or two cups of coffee prior to a road race would slightly improve performance. Caffeine is a stimulant. If it doesn't bother an individual's stomach, coffee would be a safe drink to try prior to a game or sporting event. But don't assume that if some coffee is good, more is better. Before strenuous activity, I recommend that an adult take one or two cups of coffee or, if preferred, a can or bottle or cola without the fizz (shake it well).

In regard to children, I know of no caffeine-exercise research on children, so I can't recommend it for them. However, in children many drugs work opposite from the way they do in adults. For example, sedatives occasionally cause excitement, and stimulants sometimes act as sedatives, so caffeine may have negative results.

Cigarettes

Nicotine and tars are potent cancer-causing agents that undoubtedly lead to an increased risk of cancer in the lungs, kidneys, and bladder. These agents always decrease the ability of the lungs to cleanse themselves and thus increase the risk of bronchitis and, probably, frequent colds as well. Also, they decrease lung function and capacity. Chronic bronchitis and emphysema frequently result from long-term smoking.

Anyone who smokes cigarettes is decreasing both his or her ability to perform athletically and projected length of survival. Any athlete who smokes and performs well is almost certainly in an anaerobic sport and is getting by on God-given talents. But he or she is still being cheated out of a better performance. If you don't believe this, ask the person to quit for twenty-four to forty-eight hours and then time him at any distance over 100 meters. Now ask him to honestly tell you how he feels after exercising.

Cortisone

Cortisone is a naturally occurring hormone that circulates at all times in the system of a healthy child or adult. In periods of stress or hard work, cortisone levels increase.

In cases of severe irritation and inflammation, where there is no chance of infection, cortisone injections will frequently be effective. This is a relatively safe procedure, if it is not administered into a weight-bearing joint, although it will weaken a tendon for three to six weeks. In my opinion, cortisone injections into weight-bearing joints should never be done in growing children and are rarely indicated for adults. Such injections are very rarely needed in children and young people, who are still developing. Most causes of irritation and inflammation in the young will heal with rest alone, which is far safer.

But rest is not always adequate for adults once the severe inflammatory process of either bursitis or tendinitis occurs. In such cases, cortisone injections may be beneficial. If an individual is under the age of sixteen, it is an excellent idea to have a second opinion before proceeding with a cortisone injection.

Marijuana

A few athletes swear they perform better after they have smoked marijuana, but this can't be true. Marijuana has a relaxing and calming effect that could dispel an athlete's anxiety or fear of failure and make a performance seems better than it actually was. But it won't improve the way an athlete plays.

Medically, marijuana is only given to people who suffer rare types of glaucoma.

Hormones

The male sex hormone testosterone is the anabolic steroid sometimes used by weightlifters, shotputters, decathletes, body builders, and discus men to help develop larger muscles and improve strength. Much has been written in nonmedical literature about the use of male sex hormones in both men and women. In fact, it has been charged that the recent successes of world-class European women resulted from taking these hormones.

Testosterone is a naturally-occurring hormone that women have in very low levels and men have in high levels. It causes growth, muscle development, and male sex characteristics. Those who take the drug believe that it brings an increase in bulk, or even muscle mass, with a resulting improvement in strength and possibly even anaerobic capacity. While an increase in the definition of muscle structure and the appearance of muscle mass appears to take place, a true increase in strength has never been proved a result. In addition, there is no proof that these effects are long lasting or permanent.

Taking testosterone suppresses the pituitary gland in the skull. This endocrine gland affects most body functions, and to alter its role with male steroids can be very deleterious. In addition, excess testosterone may lead to the following conditions:

1/ An increased risk of cancer, including cancer of the prostate. It has been proved that cancer grows in response to testosterone, but the exact extent of this risk is unknown. We will probably find out a lot more about it in years to come from the body builders and others who have been taking the drug.

2/ Prematurely arrested growth in adolescents. *Never* allow a healthy adolescent to take steroids.

3/ Increased facial hair, and probably chest hair, in females.

4/ Greater probability of heart attacks.

5/ Possible suppression of the function of the testes or pituitary gland, accompanied by the development of other endocrine problems.

6/ High blood pressure.

7/ Irritability.

5 / The Differences Between Men and Women in Sports

MUCH has been written about the desirability and appropriateness of equal and joint participation of the two sexes in sports, but I believe the key to the entire issue can be given in a single sentence: In sports, the only pertinent differences between men and women are a 10 percent speed and power advantage for men, and women's breasts.

On the average, the best male athletes will be 10 percent faster and more powerful than their female counterparts. This can be confirmed by a comparison of age-group records or standards of performance. For example, in spite of the fact that girls develop faster than boys and, for a while, are usually larger, the age-group time standards in running and swimming for boys eight years old and up average about 10 percent faster than comparable standards for girls. At a state, national, or international level, these differences also hold for almost any other sport. While this disparity between men and women is not absolute, it provides a rough guide that is very useful when thinking about the problems of mixed teams in any sport.

As for women's other endowments, there are countless stories on TV or in the newspapers about the best hitter on the Little League baseball team or the best goalee on the junior hockey team who was banned from play because of her sex. Invariably these girls are pre-pubescent, and as a general rule, I think girls of that age should be able to participate without restriction in any sports that are safe for boys. I see no justifiable reason for sex discrimination at that stage.

I can relate many cases of girls who masqueraded as boys in order to play a sport. One young girl even assumed another name and survived several seasons of hockey as one of the outstanding players on an all-male team. When she began to develop breasts, she changed sports because she feared the story would leak out.

The major controversy over the proper sports for women centers on the so-called contact or (more appropriately) collision sports. Probably the most important questions regarding women's participation in such sports concern the dangers of contusion and trauma to the breasts. Unfortunately, there are no real data available on the subject, although much emotional material has been printed about it.

Without question, contusions to breasts can be painful. But whether or not repeated contusions and bruising have any long-term detrimental effects, if they impair a woman's ability to nurse or make her more susceptible to cysts, is totally unproved on a scientific basis. Thus, for sports such as boxing and football, the major problem is lack of data that would substantiate or refute such harm. Nor has any appropriate breast protection been developed for these sports, but that is really a minor problem and could easily be overcome if the demand for such protection existed.

As far as I am concerned, most of the arguments regarding men versus women in sports are unsubstantiated nonsense. If one thinks about it from a purely functional point of view, the female external genitalia are actually less vulnerable in most sports situations than those of the male, which tend to require more protection.

Women are often criticized by men for being too emotional, because they tend to cry more easily. This is seen as a sign of weakness. I think an even better case can be made for tears as a sign of strength. Although tears are upsetting to most men, they may very well be a more appropriate way of handling extreme emotion or disappointment than simply "keeping it all in." Males undergo many stresses that could be relieved more therapeutically by crying than by a stoic, macho front, the sign of "taking it like a man."

Exercise usually has little or no effect on female metabolism. At times, vigorous activity may cause temporary alterations in the menstrual cycle, but there are no known permanent effects of vigorous exercise on the female reproductive system.

The reverse is not true, however. A menstrual cycle may have some adverse effects on performance if the flow of blood is exceptionally heavy. In such cases, the athlete's aerobic capacity may be somewhat diminished. That explains why many female European competitors were given birth control drugs to prevent menstruation during the 1976 Montreal Olympics.

Separate Sports?

For the benefit of those school systems or institutions that are hard-strapped to meet Title Nine (the federal regulation that requires equal opportunity in sports), there is really very little scientific reason to prevent girls and boys from practicing together. In fact, it is often quite beneficial and better for morale. Some coaches might even find practices improve with the addition of girls on a team, especially in the lower grades.

It is unfair to suppress the strong competitive urge of many females, but up until very recently there was a serious lack of organized sports available to women. Mothers who themselves were unable to compete often live out their ambitions vicariously in their children (as do many fathers who *did* have the opportunities).

Although I feel very strongly that young boys and girls can compete on equal levels, this becomes more difficult in high school, for a very simple reason: Most interscholastic teams are composed of the top 10 percent of players, ranked according to ability. In a large school, the players chosen may not even amount to 1 percent of the student body. Therefore, given the average 10 percent speed and power advantage of men over women, all but the truly exceptional woman would effectively be screened out of the competition. I believe therefore it is far better to have separate sports at that and more advanced levels. Separation of the sexes in mature athletes really encourages greater participation and fairer competition.

6 / Children and Sports

TIMES are changing! Not long ago children would just go out to a vacant lot or field and play games, with a minimum of organization and equipment. Now it seems that parents almost feel neglectful if they fail to enter their children in some organized sport soon after they have entered grammar school. Thus, the question most frequently asked by parents who bring an injured child to see me is "What sport is safe for my child?"

The final decision as to which sport your child chooses may be out of your hands by the time you are ready to make it, but early emphasis on a sport or sports that may be most appropriate for the child's size, physique, and emotional temperament can be very helpful. Unquestionably, some sports are better for certain kinds of physiques and temperaments than are others. One way to judge this is to look at your own abilities. They are usually similar to those of your child.

A word of caution: It is not appropriate for children to play with pain or to "win at all costs." It is simply not true that winning is everything; for children, participating is everything.

Organized sports are a mixed blessing for children. They certainly provide opportunity for participation in a way most parents never had. But it is unfortunate that elaborate organization and parental involvement tend to ruin a good thing. It is absolutely criminal that certain parents by court order have to be outlawed from the stands of various sports. The Little League father and the swimming mother are well-known syndromes that certainly give parenting and parental involvement in sports a black eye.

Even worse, of course, is the coach who thinks he's a Vince Lombardi, as he chews out the young children on a Little League football team. This is emotionally harmful to children, and I believe it runs counter to what sports and play are all about. Therefore, I think it is extremely important in choosing a sport to know who is going to be coaching your child. Attend a practice session or two. Listen to what is said. It is far better to pull your child out of a group early than to subject him or her to abuse that may ruin the liking for a sport forever. If you think this can't happen, you're deluding yourself.

Several studies show that the two things children dislike most about organized sports are being berated by the coach and having their parents scream and holler in the stands. Losing is a distant third to the first two objections. We can also learn something from the comments our children make to the psychiatrists and psychologists who test them. Often it is the parents who can't stand to lose, not the children. Winning and losing is all a part of life, and while winning may be more fun than losing, it certainly is not the whole reason for playing a sport or doing anything else. It is far better to enter your child in a program where everyone gets to participate, preferably in every position.

The earlier a difficult activity is learned the better it is learned, but some sports are easier than others for children at various ages. When a sport is learned naturally and well, it can be of benefit for the rest of a lifetime.

Training a Child

The athletic training of a child is an individual matter, depending on the age of the child and the particular sport. For children under the age of ten, any activity must be fun and limited in scope. It is crazy to drive children at this age. Don't force them to practice until they are dog-tired or until they quit. They may quit the sport for good. Most children innately know their limits of tolerance, and it is simply wrong to push anyone under the age of ten in any training regimen.

It is difficult to know what to say about children between the ages of ten and thirteen. What has been said about the ten year old probably applies to the preteenager as well; however, a bit of encouragement in training might not be harmful, if done in very judicious doses.

The teenage athlete can usually be trained and pushed. But remember that the rapidly growing child uses up enormous amounts of energy in the growth process alone. The more rapidly a child is growing, the more vulnerable his or her growth zones are to injury, fatigue, and pain, particularly in the knee, heel, shoulder, elbow, hip, and back. The martinet coach or parent really has no place in a child's sports activities before the years of high school, if at any time, and prior to college there is little room for the boot-camp training routine.

Parents who see a gifted athlete or future Olympic contender in their child often run to the best team in the area and uproot the whole family for the sake of the child. Or they drive the child mercilessly, harder and harder, forgetting that life for the young is supposed to be fun. It might help them—and their children—to know that many Olympic athletes did not even take up their sports until they were at least eleven or older. Sometimes the most gifted young athletes, in rebellion against their parents, totally abandon a sport when they become adolescents. Therefore, to drive a child for an occasional medal or vicarious glory is very foolish.

An Olympic-caliber athlete requires a very special combination of athletic gifts, dedication, training, and emotional qualities that do not include rebellion. Well-meaning parents who are convinced they have a gifted child and push the child without regard to enjoyment or other diversionary activities run a significant risk of souring the child early and having him or her rebel or refuse to participate further. If this happens, they have only themselves to blame.

7 / A Rating of Sporting Activities

A S a result of the current explosion in sporting activities, I am more and more frequently asked, "Doc, which sports do you recommend?"

That's a tough question because there are so many variables. Recommending some sports and not others also carries certain risks —one doesn't like to rile a 280-pound defensive tackle by giving his favorite sport a low rating. Nonetheless, I have attempted to rank the most popular sporting activities, not on grounds of personal preference, but in terms of physiological benefit, safety, and cost.

To do this, I weighed each sport's physiological value for overall conditioning, emphasizing aerobic activities rather than anaerobic events (see page 13). As a physician I must rate the aerobic sports higher than those that are anaerobic. I also gave preference to those sports that are safest. Then, I judged the overall cost of the activity to the participant, parent, or school. In most cases a sport that is less expensive is ranked higher than one that is more expensive, if all other elements are about the same. In addition to comments on the sport itself, I have sometimes mentioned certain attributes that will help a man, woman, or child more fully develop or enjoy it. Finally, my ranking only concerns participation in a sport, not the way it looks from a spectator's point of view.

1/ Cross-country, jogging, and track. Without question, running is the safest sport of all; it gives the best conditioning for the money, and it is available year-round in almost any climate. The only conditions that may preclude running are ice storms or excessive heat (90°F with 90 percent humidity). The spiritual, physical, and psychological benefits of running are also substantial, and it can be a lifelong activity. Men over thirty and women over forty should have a physician's okay to begin.

Any school, regardless of its financial situation, can institute a jogging or cross-country program, because no special facilities are needed for it. Body size is neither an advantage nor a disadvantage in cross-country, but most runners are not big people. If one has a very large build or tends to be heavy, this might not be the ideal sport, but it will eventually trim off excess fat. Jogging is a superb recreational activity for anyone. Track is included in my list because it requires excellent aerobic training, although 400-meter dashes or less are considered anaerobic events.

Though jogging should be a safe sport, accidents happen, mostly at sunrise and sunset when visibility is poor. Occasionally joggers are killed by automobiles, or even trains. It is wise to run scared on the road, as if every car might hit you. You should carry a flashlight at night. In true cross-country activity, sprained and broken ankles sometimes occur on rough grades.

Marathons (twenty-six-mile-long distance runs) are a part of cross-country running, but they make abnormal demands on the body. The "wall" that marathoners speak of occurs in most runners at the distance of about eighteen to nineteen miles. It is a total depletion of the body's energy stores. Theoretically it is impossible to run a marathon without taking in supplemental nourishment to prevent the breakdown of body tissues for energy. Therefore, only a well-trained individual should attempt a marathon; running one on a dare could be dangerous, and it might take three months for an untrained body to recuperate. A well-conditioned jogger requires a minimum of three to six months of special training to finish a marathon. If you are not a jogger or a runner, a maximum of fifteen miles (twenty-five kilometers) may be attempted, but longer distances can be quite harmful. Someone who is out of shape should not attempt a marathon without a year of training. It could be a very regrettable experience.

2/ Cross-country skiing. This is the single best exercise activity available to modern man. Obviously the sport has limitations of climate and season, but as an overall fitness activity and a beautiful way to see a winter landscape it is unsurpassed.

Cross-country skiing is considered by many to be a perfectly safe sport, but it isn't. Injuries do occur, mostly when going down icy slopes, and they can be serious. This sport is not recommended for people with heart trouble who are not in excellent condition and have not been cleared by a physician. It is not recommended for asthmatics.

3/ Competitive swimming. The greatest drawbacks of swimming are lack of facilities and cost. It is generally a safe sport that involves only mild shoulder and knee injuries and an occasional back problem among those who do the butterfly stroke. Another common injury that occurs in competitive swimming is a cut heel from doing flip turns at the end of a pool. A number of deaths occur in recreational swimming, but the statistics do not sort out diving from swimming injuries. Also, boating accidents are lumped together with the swimming statistics. Deaths associated with diving in shallow water are probably a significant factor, but competitive swimming is exceedingly safe.

Swimming is second to cross-country skiing as an overall exercise and muscle development sport, but for the trained swimmer it is not as good as jogging in terms of aerobic exercise. Anyone who is untrained would probably profit equally from swimming and jogging. Ironically, the better one swims, the faster one has to swim to receive a training benefit.

Swimming is an excellent sport to recommend for a child who is somewhat overweight. The penalty for being overweight counts less in this sport due to the water's buoyancy, so heavy children can compete on a nearly equal level with others. In fact, there may be some value to being a little overweight, since extra fat adds buoyancy.

Swimming is absolutely the best sport for asthmatics. An asthmatic child, under a doctor's direction, should be strongly encouraged to swim. Dr. Kenneth Fitch, who was the team physician for the Australian Olympic team, has gone so far as to say "A swim a day keeps the asthma away." Not long ago, virtually one-third to one-half of the players on the Australian Olympic swimming team were asthmatics. In Australia there is a vigorous program to get asthmatics into swimming at an early age because it is so good for them. It is one competitive sport where exercise-induced asthma is minimal.

In my experience, children with learning disabilities are also helped significantly by swimming. They do better in school and behave better as a result of the sport.

Competitive swimming is available to almost any child above the age of six and to any adult, now that an active Masters program has been started by the YMCA and the Amateur Athletic Union (AAU). Swimming teaches the lesson of losing as well as winning, and instills an appreciation of the rewards of practice. It also teaches parents and children to set achievable goals, since performances can be measured by time rather than by beating other competitors. From that standpoint, the sport is invaluable.

On a competitive basis, the better one gets the more time one must spend in a pool. At present, top level swimmers may train as much as four or five hours a day. In terms of time, swimming on the competition level is one of the most demanding sports, which explains why many swimmers simply get soured on it and quit it for good.

4/ Soccer. Fortunately, soccer is catching on in the United States. It is a wonderful team sport that is an excellent conditioner and requires a minimum of equipment and expense. Also, young children can learn the skills naturally, without the need for coaching. Size is neither an advantage nor a disadvantage in the game, although speed and agility are obviously useful assets.

Major knee-ligament injuries are virtually nonexistent in soccer as long as the sport is played in bare feet or noncleated shoes, although minor knee injuries are common. When spikes are worn knee injuries do occur, but they do not happen as frequently as in football. Broken legs are rare.

In these days of general financial pressure, it is almost inexcusable for any school, from the grammar level through college, not to offer soccer. Unfortunately, in some areas of the country, large groups of young athletes are denied a sport in the fall because their only alternatives are football or cross-country.

5/ Basketball. Basketball is an excellent conditioning sport if played on a full court. In terms of the number of players participating, it has been the national sport for many years, although for some reason people have refused to admit it. The chief problem with basketball is that a player's size is a distinct factor at almost any level, so those who are unusually tall and agile should be encouraged to play it.

For overall cost and safety, basketball is an excellent sport. Sprained ankles and finger injuries are the usual problems, although some knee ligament damage may also occur in older players. At the collegiate and pro levels, where size gets to be significant and large bodies start bumping into one another, more injuries arise.

6/ Cycling. As an overall conditioning activity, especially for the heart, cycling is superb. It is also an excellent family activity. But as a competitive sport at the scholastic level, cycling is virtually nonexistent, and club-level cycling is available in only limited areas. Olympic cycling is helping the growth of this sport, although there are very few places for indoor cycling in North America.

Intensive studies of bicycle injuries show that most accidents occur when two people ride the same bike. Bicycle spoke injuries to the heel are vicious because they heal poorly, can cause permanent or prolonged damage, and often leave a permanent scar. Helmets are necessary for cyclists who ride at high speeds and are recommended for cycling on roads because cars cause a lot of injuries in this sport. It is also dangerous to cycle on gravel roads and to ride in the rain with handbrakes, since wet handbrakes function poorly, if at all.

7/ Racquetball, handball, and squash. Racquetball is a very good game that is easily learned and provides a great deal of excellent aerobic exercise. Goggles should be mandatory, especially in doubles, since a racquetball fits almost perfectly into the human eye socket, and it is small enough to hit the eyeball directly. Except for eye injuries and an occasional case of Achilles tendinitis or a hit from a racquet, this sport is safe. The sore shoulder that develops in many racquetball players is due to lack of proper wrist action.

What has been said about racquetball applies equally well to handball and squash, except of course goggles are not as necessary in those sports. Also, racquetball and squash are easier on the hands than handball.

8/ Tennis. Tennis is an excellent game that children should start early in order to develop the proper skills. The problem with tennis for the average hacker over twenty-five is the difficulty of becoming good enough to get adequate exercise from the sport. Until one advances to the B level, it is hard to get much exercise out of tennis, so, in general, it should not be considered a conditioning sport.

With proper training and conditioning, tennis is very safe. The major problems that develop involve the elbow, Achilles tendon (in players over thirty-five), and, occasionally, the shoulder. Any adult who wants to take up tennis should have a pain-free back.

9/ Speed and figure skating. Speed skating is an excellent conditioning sport, although it is not readily available. A good surface is an absolute prerequisite, since skates can catch in ice cracks, causing injuries. Figure skating is equally beneficial and more available, but, unfortunately, it can be very expensive.

10/ Crew, rowing, and kayaking. For overall conditioning, training, endurance, and strength and body development, crew and the various rowing sports are almost without peer, although the opportunities for doing them are somewhat limited. They are also excellent sports for athletes with exercise-induced asthma. Injuries are rare.

11/ Wrestling. Strains, bumps, and shoulder separations are common wrestling injuries, and knee injuries occur occasionally. On the whole, wrestling is a rough sport, but not really dangerous. Wrestlers are usually very well conditioned and build up excellent bodies. Participants should have a fairly high pain tolerance, however.

The biggest problem in wrestling is "making" (losing) weight. Unfortunately, the weight classifications for wrestlers do not correspond very closely to the weight spreads of the population. Instead, the classifications favor people at either end of the size spectrum. Thus, if a boy is very small or very large, wrestling may be an excellent sport for him.

As a general rule, it is extremely unsafe and potentially dangerous for any athlete to try to lose more than 10 percent of his body weight to qualify in a weight category. It is very unwise for a rapidly growing thin boy to lose any weight at all, but for others, 10 percent is a fairly safe guideline. Any more than that is asking for defeat in the next meet or even serious medical complications. The really good wrestlers in any age category have very little difficulty in making weight. This puts those who do have such problems at a disadvantage because their bodies may be half-starved or fatigued.

Any camp a child attends should insist on the wearing of headgear (ear protectors) at all times while wrestling. A wrestler who doesn't wear headgear may get cauliflower ears.

12/ Field hockey and lacrosse. These sports tend to be a combination between soccer and hockey. They are excellent conditioning sports, and were it not for the sticks and clubs in people's hands, they would be quite safe. Of the two, field hockey is by far the safest.

13/ Volleyball. Volleyball is an excellent team sport that requires some conditioning. But finger injuries are common, and if a child has chondromalacia (see page 83), it is probably one of the worst sports to play because it will aggravate this condition.

14/ Judo and martial arts. Judo (Japanese for "gentle art") is valuable training experience for preadolescents. It teaches the proper techniques of falling, which can be an invaluable aid in almost any activity.

Although it is valuable for individuals of all ages, I think judo is best for unaggressive children, both male and female. As judo is mainly a defensive activity, it will not make a child aggressive, but it may build confidence in some stressful situations.

Karate and other martial arts are more aggressive than judo. They are easy and not stressful for children, but they can be a vigorous undertaking for a grown adult who is not experienced in falling, or who is out of condition.

15/ Baseball. It is difficult to know where to put baseball. Little League elbow has given baseball, certainly at the junior-high level and below, a bad reputation. But baseball is an extremely safe sport, especially since the advent of batting helmets. However, baseball is not demanding as a conditioning sport and should really be thought of as a game. If a child has quick reflexes and excellent hand-eye coordination, baseball should be considered.

16/ Scuba diving. The initials of scuba stand for self-contained underwater breathing apparatus. Scuba diving is potentially quite dangerous; injuries in this sport can lead to paralysis and death. Fortunately, the injury rate is kept quite low in the United States by a regulation that limits the dispensing of compressed air only to certified scuba divers.

For learning scuba, the courses given by the YMCA and other certified scuba-instruction classes are very good. Part of the training involves good conditioning. This is especially stressed at the YMCA.

Never attempt to do any scuba diving before passing a certified scuba course. To do so is risky and foolish. Unless you know what you are doing, you may die—or end up permanently paralyzed with brain damage. Avoid any short, ''crash'' courses in scuba diving; that kind of preparation is totally inadequate.

By contrast, snorkeling is very safe, as long as a swimmer realizes the sun's tanning rays can penetrate three feet into the water.

17/ Downhill skiing. As an aerobic activity, downhill skiing rates far higher than baseball, but I placed it lower due to the risk of injury and cost. The risks in downhill skiing are well documented, but an exact safety factor cannot be determined, since statistics are not available in the United States. Certainly one should be in good condition for downhill skiing. This sport is best learned at an early age, and the GLM, or Graduated Length Method, is a fairly safe way to begin. In my opinion, the number of ski injuries among beginners has decreased with the introduction of GLM instruction. Tibia fractures still occur, but knee-ligament injuries are becoming more common as boots, bindings, and skis change.

One of the most serious injuries is a slow healing, nasty fracture of the tibia, called a boot-top fracture. It is often caused by ski bindings. In fact, the majority of injuries that occur on ski slopes are either the result of a faulty setting of bindings or faulty bindings.

18/ Golf. Golf is a very frustrating game and its skills are best learned early. It provides a good walk and fresh air, but minimal conditioning. If golf weren't so expensive, I would rate it higher than baseball.

19/ Field events. With the exception of pole-vaulting, field is generally a fairly safe endeavor, although occasionally someone is hit in the head with a shot put or stabbed with a javelin. Proper coaching techniques are obviously of value. Most people are capable of doing some track or field event.

20/ Gymnastics. Injuries in men's gymnastics are not very common. Most injuries are sprained ankles that occur during tumbling routines or falls from the rings. The biggest risk in men's gymnastics is a fall following a giant turn and flyaway on the high bar.

Women gymnasts seem to be more prone than men gymnasts to injury. One study indicates that 10 percent of competitive female gymnasts will develop significant back problems. Back pain or the development of tight hamstrings in female gymnasts really demand medical attention and should not be ignored. In addition, falls off the balance beam and dismounts that are out of control can lead to serious knee and ankle injuries, as well as to occasional elbow problems. The uneven parallel bars provide much the same risk that the high bar does in men's gymnastics, but the balance beam is really the biggest offender. In gym classes, many girls attempt to do balance beam maneuvers that are beyond their capability, not realizing the risks involved. Gymnastics certainly cannot be thought of as a safe sport, but if a child is flexible and agile, it might be a good one.

21/ Football. As far as danger is concerned, football is a contact, or collision, sport, so injuries are to be expected in the game. The only accurate statistics available on football injuries come from the NFL, which reports a 90 percent injury rate per year. This means that every year, 90 percent of all the players in the NFL will have a significant injury of some sort. Not included in these figures are many of the common finger injuries, deep and superficial bruises, ankle sprains, and neck problems, which would be considered disabling injuries in other sports, but are ignored by football players. I know of one boy who hid a paralyzed arm for three games.

The rewards of football can be great, however, both financially and socially. At the high school and collegiate levels, football still attracts most of the best athletes, and it accounts for most of the sports scholarships. Size, speed, and a high pain tolerance are all favorable attributes for participation in the game. In turn, the sport develops aggressiveness and the ability to sacrifice for a common goal, work hard, and play as part of a team. Perhaps that is why so many business executives are ex-football players.

At the high-school level, proper conditioning and coaching help decrease injuries, which occur mostly during the first half of the season. Aerobic conditioning seems to decrease injuries at any level, however, as does weight training and lack of fatigue. The probability of injury is also less under wet or icy conditions, when cleats cannot hold the ground well. It takes a foot firmly planted in the ground to cause a significant knee injury.

22/ Hockey. Now that complete face guards are mandatory in the United States for hockey players in grades below the high school level, the frequent loss of eyes has stopped, as have most serious facial injuries. The major hazards in hockey are hits by a stick or puck. If it were not for the stick, hockey would be a very safe sport at the junior level. Two other drawbacks to hockey are its expense and the late hours of team games that cut into normal sleeping time.

At the high-school and college levels, collisions with the boards and hits from sticks are the primary causes of injuries. Hockey is a rough sport, and it is foolish not to wear a complete face guard when playing the game. Unorganized hockey may be even more dangerous than school hockey, because the players often fail to wear face guards.

23/ Horseback riding. Many people consider horseback riding to be one of the truly dangerous sports, and rightfully so. Many deaths and serious injuries do occur to horseback riders, although enthusiasts of the sport will deny this vehemently. Anytime I treat an injured horseman, the first thing he or she does is defend the horse. But, no matter who is to blame, there is a significant national incidence of deaths associated with horseback riding as well as horse racing, so it must be considered a dangerous pastime.

24/ Bowling. Bowling is almost worthless for conditioning, but it is better than sitting and watching television and does require some skill.

25/ Skateboards. Recent studies indicate that skateboards have a significantly higher injury rate than motorcycles. This is because skateboards are more accessible than motorcycles, and children can start using them quite young. If a child insists on having a skateboard, then a helmet, elbow and knee pads, and gloves should be mandatory. Many deaths and serious head injuries have occurred on skateboards and, unfortunately, will probably continue to do so as a result of the sport's popularity. Severe deep abrasions, or floor burns, are common in skateboarding.

26/ Boxing. A boxer receives superior aerobic conditioning as well as some anaerobic training. Skipping rope, road work, and various other exercises associated with the sport are all excellent conditioning activities, and, indeed, boxing was one of the first sports to recognize the value of aerobic training. In addition, boxing teaches self-defense, which many people consider valuable.

Although the training and conditioning of a boxer are excellent, it is difficult for a physician to approve of the sport because its ultimate goal is a knockout—or, in essence, the infliction of brain damage. If one must participate, headgear should be worn.

27/ Motorcycling and minibiking. Riding any kind of motorcycle or minibike, either on or off the street, is extremely hazardous. Automobile drivers frequently do not see motorcycles on the road and may broadside them or run them off the pavement, intentionally or unintentionally. Motorcycles are also dangerous on wet or gravel roads. When driven by someone who is under the influence of alcohol, a motorcycle can be suicidal.

Minibikes are really small motorcycles. They are purchased for children by well-meaning parents who have been deluded into thinking they are safe. On the contrary, minibikes are extremely dangerous, and many severe or fatal injuries have occurred on them. The problem with these small motorcycles is that children have no concept of what speed can do and they misjudge it, even if they seem responsible and have a lot of common sense. The only thing that's more dangerous than a child on a minibike is an adult on one; minibikes are very unstable.

The supporters of motorcycling have basically come to agree that on public thoroughfares the activity is dangerous. Mopeds involve the same hazards, by the way. Orthopedic surgeons and neurosurgeons have seen so much carnage from motorcycle and minibike accidents that they have difficulty even being sympathetic with the victims.

Never ride a motorcycle, motorbike, or minibike with bare legs or feet. Slides and falls on these vehicles can badly tear and scar the legs.

28/ Snowmobiling. Snowmobiles tend to be more dangerous than motorcycles because a certain craziness seems to come over people who get on them. Drownings and frostbite incidents are numerous from driving snowmobiles over unseen lakes or streams that are inadequately frozen, or from overexposure and windchill. Decapitations from barbed-wire fences and horrible facial and throat lacerations are also common among snowmobilers. Drinking alcohol magnifies the dangers of speed and misjudgment in this activity.

29/ Trampoline. The American Academy of Pediatrics has condemned the trampoline and recommended that its use be banned from all schools. I concur with them. Trampolinists experience a significant rate of neck injury that often results in permanent paralysis. Proponents of the trampoline think that it is safe if used with proper spotting and feel it is the best way to teach spatial relationships and special gymnastic and diving movements to children. A spotter is someone who is supposed to stand by the trampoline and prevent the trampolinist from injury. But even with proper spotting, serious injuries do occur —this is certainly too high a price to pay for having a trampoline in regular gym classes.

Even for teaching specific diving techniques or gymnastic routines the risks seem too high. Also, competitive trampoline activity, where available, can lead to repetitive stresses and problems in the back. In brief, I do not recommend the sport at all.

30/ Freestyle skiing. Another extremely dangerous sport is "hot-dogging," acrobatic skiing complete with somersaults. This incredibly dangerous sport, although glamorized on television, is not for the novice. Participants of this activity experience an extremely high rate of broken necks and paralysis, and I do not recommend it.

31/ Hang gliding. The distinction of most dangerous sporting activity probably belongs to hang gliding. Although statistics are not available on the subject, hang gliding no doubt has the highest incidence of serious fractures, fractures complicated by paralysis, and death of any sport. Needless to say, it is not recommended.

Part Two

Sports Injuries and Problems

8 / How to Evaluate an Injury

THERE is an appropriate way to evaluate every injury or painful condition. To help you do this, I have carefully outlined the steps that will enable you to understand a problem and communicate it to your physician. This subject is so important that an entire chapter is devoted to it. With such knowledge, you may be able to avoid a long, unnecessary wait in an emergency room—or you may save yourself a real disability by promptly seeking the right care.

Determining the Seriousness of Injury

There are three steps to take in evaluating every injury: ask about it; look at it; touch it.

1/ Ask questions about the injury. How did it occur? Did it stop participation? How much does it hurt, and does it hurt more now than when it happened? Injuries that were the result of a relatively minor force are usually less significant than those caused by a strong one. If an injured child stopped playing immediately, it usually indicates a more severe hurt than if play continued. If pain decreases within several hours after the accident, chances are the problem is not serious, but if it gets worse, a serious injury might exist.

2/ Look at the injury. The injured part must be identified exactly, so don't just accept "arm." Ask the athlete to point to the exact area, and then remove any clothing to look at it directly. The procedure for removing a garment from an injured limb is to clear the normal arm or leg first and then the injured member. Conversely, if you're covering up an injury, it's easier to start with the injured part first, since the normal part can move more freely. In other words, as far as clothing is concerned, an injured limb should be "last out and first in."

In looking at an injury, see if there is any obvious deformity. Is there any subtle swelling? Is there any bruising? Again, be sure you know exactly where it hurts. See if the injured arm or leg can be moved by the athlete. If both arm and hand or leg and foot can be moved freely and painlessly, then the injury is obviously less serious than if the person is unable or unwilling to move the painful part. If there is only subtle swelling and you're still not sure what to think, then go to the next step.

3/ Palpate or gently touch the injured area. If there is no obvious swelling or deformity, touching the area is not likely to do any harm. Children and athletes are not china dolls; as a general rule, they are quite tough, so you can touch an injury gently but firmly to find out if there is tenderness around it. If the whole arm or leg can be touched or softly squeezed, and you find no area of tenderness, the chances of having a subtle fracture are remote. In children under the age of twelve, however, there probably is a minor fracture if questionable swelling and tenderness on the bone persist after applying ice packs for five or six hours. The tenderness of a fracture will not go away in twenty-four hours and the swelling may even grow if the application of ice has been inadequate.

Sprains in children under the age of twelve are rare: their ligaments are stronger than their bones, so the bones will go first. In a child, any injury that is accompanied by swelling and bruising around a joint is probably a fracture, until proved otherwise by an expert. Most fractures will heal without difficulty, but certain ones can doom a joint to permanent disability. This can be prevented by early diagnosis and surgery, so don't ever ignore a significant injury to a child under the misguided belief that it is "only a sprain."

The steps outlined above also apply to moderate injury, but severe injuries are handled differently. Severe injury is indicated when a person is unable to move an arm, or to walk or get around.

If an arm is hurt and the deformity or pain is not great, then it is safe to gently lift it with both hands and rest it in a sling or on a pillow. The injured person can then be transported to a doctor's office or the nearest emergency room.

For a leg injury with marked deformity or pain, especially if the foot is twisted out at an abnormal angle, it is best to send for professional help in moving the person. Chances of a major fracture of the leg are great and the risk of doing more harm by lifting and transporting the individual is significant. It is better to leave this to professionals. There is no harm in letting someone who is having no difficulty breathing lie still for a few more minutes until help comes. Cover the person with a blanket, if possible. If there is no head or neck injury or pain in those areas, you may cradle the individual or give him a small pillow.

Never give a seriously injured person anything to eat or drink, not even a sip of water, until he or she has been cleared by an emergency-room physician. To feed anyone with marked swelling or an obvious deformity of an arm or a leg before he or she is given a medical examination can lead to grave consequences if an anesthetic must be used.

Degrees of Pain

Throughout the book I will speak of mild, moderate, and severe pain. The following tips will help you classify the degree of pain and sort out the serious complaints from those that are minor.

Mild pain does not stop a person from participating in a sport and, frequently, is not present during the activity. The pain will develop as movement slows down. Usually, this type of pain can be completely relieved by aspirin or by an ice pack applied to the area that hurts. Mild pain never interrupts sleep; and it does not keep one awake at night.

Moderate pain may not stop one's participation, but it is usually present while a person is active, and it frequently impedes performance. Aspirin may relieve the pain, but normally will only lessen it. Ice will also provide some (but not complete) relief. Moderate pain does not necessarily interrupt sleep, but it may occasionally waken a person, especially when an injured part is moved or becomes twisted the wrong way during sleep.

Severe pain brings all activity with the injured part to a complete halt. The pain is not relieved by aspirin; ice only helps deaden it; and sleep is often difficult and interrupted.

Reactions to pain can vary, however. The behavior of a suffering person is called a ''pain behavior,'' and it is learned from one's culture or environment. This is one reason for paying particular attention to children. We must look carefully at how injuries affect adolescents, not at how they react, since they may not have had sufficient time to learn their cultural norm for pain behavior. One extreme is seen in the behavior of the Chinese or in American Indians who are very stoic and show little or no reaction to many severely painful injuries. In contrast, southern European or South American people sometimes react dramatically to relatively minor problems.

As a general rule, it's safe to believe children when they say they hurt and when they complain. However, to judge the severity of their pain, watch their behavior. If in a few minutes they've forgotten the complaint, it would rate as a minor problem. If they are limping or not using an arm or leg, or refusing to do so, a more severe problem is indicated. Frequently children with significant problems do not complain of pain at all, but simply fail to use the injured part. On the other hand, a dramatic child can be quite vociferous in reacting to minor pain but resume playing at full speed five minutes later.

Vocalizations of pain in adults and teenagers can have a different meaning, however. A relatively minor problem may be complained of bitterly to achieve a conscious or unconscious goal. Many minor joint complaints or "incurable" conditions can be solved by temporarily eliminating an activity that a teenager wants to avoid. Sometimes the only honorable way to get out of a sporting activity, even for a mature person, is to claim an injury. It is always best to observe how closely a complaint correlates to a specific activity, if there is any question about its seriousness.

Heat

Heat will increase swelling around an injury and may actually be harmful. If heat is applied to an injury within the first twenty-four hours, or even up to seventy-two hours, it will frequently prolong the recovery period. Remember, it's always safe to apply ice—but never heat.

Under the right circumstances, heat can be soothing, and will help to reduce stiffness. Sometimes it is also used alternately with ice, under a doctor's guidance, to rehabilitate an injury, but it should never be employed for an acute injury.

Ice: The Universal Drug

A general rule of sports medicine is that ice is the "drug" of choice in almost all injuries except frostbite, as long as there is no break in the skin. Ice does many things—all of which are good. It cools the injured area and will prevent and reduce swelling. It reduces pain and it promotes healing. In the following chapters, when an ice pack is recommended, it should be applied for fifteen- to twenty-minute periods, three to five times a day.

There are three basic types of ice pack. The most convenient is a plastic bag or commercially made ice bag filled with crushed ice. But most trainers freeze water in paper or styrofoam cups that can easily be held and rubbed on the injured part for a period of ten to fifteen minutes, or as frequently as is comfortable. Commercially made cold packs are also available in sporting good stores, and they work, too, but nothing surpasses old-fashioned ice for effectiveness.

Taping

Taping usually gives an athlete a false sense of security and too often becomes a crutch. The stability of a limb or joint really depends on proper exercise and strengthening of the muscles. Taping of the ankles may have some benefit (see page 71), but it is virtually of no use for the knee, because movement of the joint works the tape loose very quickly. The same is true of tape on the arm or hand.

Elastic tape should be used only with caution during an activity, because it can become too constricting. Its purpose is really to keep swelling down in certain injuries while a person is inactive. Conversely, tape that is too tight will cause swelling, so any taping must be done judiciously.

Leg and Arm Pains in Children and Adolescents

Occasional episodes of leg cramps or pain are a common occurrence in children and teenagers and may even waken them during the night or make them cry. Such cramps are relieved with massage, which should permit the youth to get back to sleep without difficulty. As long as such cramps are intermittent, medical evaluation will probably not be helpful. But if they occur nightly or consistently, professional advice should be sought.

Painless limping that lasts for more than a day in a child warrants an orthopedic evaluation. If there is no tenderness in the foot, ankle, or leg, the child may have a serious hip or knee problem that can develop insidiously. Never ignore a limp that lasts more than twenty-four to forty-eight hours.

The same holds true for adolescents, although the problem may be different. Rapidly growing teenagers are subject to a condition called slipped epiphysis, which can make them increasingly duck-footed on one or both sides. This proclivity may indicate a severe hip problem that will require orthopedic treatment, perhaps surgery. Do not ignore a limp or, especially, the progressive turning-out of a foot in a teenager. An orthopedic evaluation should be made within twenty-four hours of the discovery of this condition.

Don't ignore an arm problem, either. Failure to use an arm is usually an indication of injury. The only time children imitate or pretend something is wrong is on the rare occasion when they mimic someone else.

Some Basic Medical Definitions

In the following chapters you will find certain terms repeated frequently. Reviewing a few definitions will help you to understand them and communicate with medical personnel.

Fracture "Fracture" is the proper medical term to describe any broken bone; a broken bone and a fracture are one and the same thing. A bone chip fracture results when two bones hit each other, usually in a joint, or when a tendon or ligament pulls a small piece of bone from the main bone structure. If a tendon or ligament is involved, the injury is also known as a pull-off fracture, and it may pertain to a large piece of bone as well as a chip. A stress, or fatigue, fracture occurs from repetitive stress or overuse that exceeds the tolerance of a bone. In an open fracture, the bone actually protrudes from the skin.

Growth Zone The growth of a bone occurs at each end in a zone called the epiphysis. These growth zones close upon maturity and do not exist in adults. An apophysis is a specialized growth zone to which a tendon is attached, somewhere between the ends of the bone.

Inflammation   Heat, redness, and swelling are indications of the body's attempt to heal any injury. Whether the harm is from a blow or an infection, the body's response is to shift a large number of white blood cells and various other chemicals to the problem area. This results in increased warmth or redness, usually accompanied by some pain and tenderness in the affected area. The four letters "itis" after a word signify inflammation, as in appendicitis or tendinitis.

Ligament   A specialized type of fibrous tissue that holds bones and joints together is known as a ligament.

Overuse Syndrome   This term is being used more and more to designate a number of conditions in athletes of all ages who are simply overusing different parts of their bodies.

Overuse in children frequently leads to painful problems that stop the activity. But with adequate rest, a child will mend. Unless they are forced by adults (i.e., coaches or overdemanding parents), children will not willfully submit to pain; they simply do something else to entertain themselves until it goes away.

Unfortunately, adults seem to lack an innate common sense that children possess. For some reason, they feel obliged to continue a sporting endeavor, in spite of developing pain in the heel, elbow, shoulder, or elsewhere. They often push themselves until the pain becomes more and more disabling and only then seek some sort of medical advice, which they will follow—with the exception of resting the injury.

This, of course, is the difficult part of treating adults for painful conditions resulting from overuse. If the painful area had been rested when the condition was minor, it would probably have healed without any permanent disability. Instead, the disregard for pain may lead to prolonged disability and frustration with the medical-care system. Even worse, the individual's performance level may drop considerably, or the favorite sport may have to be abandoned altogether.

The problem in adults is further complicated by tissues that are less flexible than a child's and ligaments and tendons that do not heal as well. In addition, aging or degeneration increases vulnerability to injury. When a joint or an area of anatomy has been abused for years, it can be virtually impossible to restore its normal function.

Sprain A sprain is any injury to a ligament. It can range from mild stress that does not weaken the ligament to a complete tear. Both extremes are medically classified as sprains, though sprains are usually divided into three grades: A grade 1 sprain is simply a minor stretch of a ligament that does not weaken it mechanically, but causes some pain and tenderness in the area. A grade 2 sprain involves a partial tear that significantly weakens the ligament, and a grade 3 sprain refers to a completely torn or ruptured ligament. Pain in both grade 2 and 3 sprains is considerable.

Tendons Tendons consist of another specialized type of fibrous tissue that connects muscles to bones. They react quickly to injury and are very sensitive, so that even minor problems will cause them to swell and become inflamed. The combination of swelling and inflammation is responsible for the painful condition called tendinitis, which can occur in any tendon of the body.

9 / Feet and Ankles

Injuries to the Toes

A COMMON toe injury is the loosening of a toenail by constant rubbing against the front of a sport shoe in the course of vigorous exercise. This problem does not usually require medical care, especially if the soreness goes away in twenty-four to forty-eight hours. If the nail does come off, the nail bed will normally cease being tender in twenty-four hours and no loss of function will occur; the nail should grow back in about three months. Both distance running and sports with sudden stops and starts, such as basketball and tennis, can cause toenails to come loose. Even with the best of care, a toenail may loosen, but keeping all nails trimmed as short as possible reduces the possibility of its happening.

The most common injury to the lesser four toes is a fracture, most frequently caused by kicking against something hard in bare feet. Usually the diagnosis is made easy by marked tenderness and bruising. If the toe appears almost normal, as in Illustration 1, the standard medical treatment is to insert a small piece of cotton between the broken toe and an adjoining one and tape the two together. You can do this yourself. If the toe is straight and not too painful, taping is not necessary. In fact, I have given great relief to many patients by removing the tape from their fractured toes. Broken toes often swell, causing the tape to become quite constricting, so the best thing in such cases is to cut off the tape.

This type of toe fracture will be moderately painful for approximately two or three weeks but should heal without difficulty. *Caution:* if the toe is abnormally angled in any direction, is numb, or has poor circulation, then emergency treatment is necessary. Explain the symp-

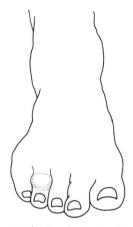

1/Fractured toe. An injury to the toe that makes it swell, as above, is probably a simple fracture.

toms to your doctor by phone immediately, and, if you cannot reach him or her, go to the emergency room at once.

Calluses

Painful calluses in the metatarsal region (ball of the foot) are the most common foot problem. A callus is easily distinguished from a plantar wart (see below) by the normal skin creases and lines running through it; these are missing in a wart.

Troublesome or painful calluses are attributed to the angle of one of the metatarsal (long) bones in the foot. The bone will tend to angle down slightly more than the other metatarsals, causing greater pressure on the bottom of the foot and, thus, the callus.

If calluses become too thick to sand down with an emery board, then it's best to have a podiatrist shave them with a scalpel. Shaving must be done with care to avoid cutting the skin. A word of caution: This type of foot problem in diabetics is extremely difficult to treat and should be taken care of by a physician.

If shaving fails to correct the problem, then a metatarsal pad or a custom-made orthosis (specialized insert) may be necessary to relieve pressure. Plastic is frequently used, and occasionally some of the new polyurethanes, such as those in custom-made ski boots, are very effective. These can be obtained from a custom shoemaker, a podiatrist, or an orthopedic surgeon who cares for common foot problems.

Conservative measures are by far the best treatment. Only if all else fails should surgery be considered, because correction of one metatarsal frequently leads to abnormal pressure on another one. The situation can resemble a dog chasing its tail.

Plantar Warts

Actually, plantar warts can occur anywhere on the foot, but they are commonly found in the metatarsal area. They are frequently mistaken for calluses, but can be distinguished from them by a lack of normal skin lines and by sensitivity when squeezed at the sides. A wart is a raised area of bumpy, thickened skin, sometimes spotted in the center with small black dots.

Warts are the result of a viral infection in the skin, and until the infection is eliminated, shaving and even surgical removal may provide only temporary relief.

Children's warts commonly respond to medications provided by most pediatricians or family practitioners, but adults are often much more difficult to treat. I usually recommend the acid preparations commonly prescribed by physicians. If these fail, then treatment by a dermatologist should be sought. If the wart still fails to respond and the pain persists, surgical removal can be attempted, but it should be the last resort, since warts will frequently recur.

Shooting Pains

Sometimes pain will shoot or radiate in between or into any of the lesser toes, most commonly the third and fourth. Typically, this pain starts after prolonged walking or running, and, when severe, relief is obtained only by stopping, taking off the shoe, and rubbing the foot.

This pain syndrome is called Morton's toe or Morton's neuroma. It is caused by an abnormal swelling and increased size in the sensory nerve to the toes between the metatarsal bones in the foot. A commercially available metatarsal pad may give some relief, but this specific type of problem usually requires surgical removal of the nerve for lasting comfort.

Arches

The height of the arch varies tremendously in children and it is not even discernible in babies under two years old because fat obscures it. If it becomes obvious that a child has a completely flat foot, an evaluation by a physician (who may recommend consulting an orthopedic surgeon) is warranted. Any complaint of foot pain by a child is uncommon, and should be investigated by a physician.

Arches in adults are an entirely different story. Commonly, the very highly arched foot is more of a problem than a flat foot because the angle of the bones causes abnormal pressure in the ball-of-the-foot area. This can lead to calluses and other problems. At the opposite extreme, many great athletes, including some Olympic medalists, have feet as flat as pancakes. As a general rule, feet that don't hurt are no problem. There are many variations in normal anatomy, and arch height is one of them.

Recurring shin splints (see page 74) in an athlete with flat feet may be caused by leg muscles attempting to support a collapsed arch. Soft arch supports or an orthosis may help alleviate this type of shin splint.

Pain Between the Ankle and the Toes

With no knowledge of an injury, people sometimes feel pain in the area between the ankle and the toes. Any part of the area may be tender, or there may be no tenderness at all. The complaint might be, "My foot only hurts when I run. If I don't run or don't walk far, it's not painful." This pain may continue for several weeks and be extremely frustrating.

First ask yourself three important questions: Has the pain developed after an especially long bout of running? Has the amount of running, jumping, or walking been increased markedly? Has the surface of the workout area been changed? If the answer to any of these questions is yes, you may have a stress fracture.

The old term for stress fracture is "march" fracture. It originated when army recruits were sent on forced forty-mile marches. A certain number of them would develop a severe, disabling foot pain, but X rays taken at the onset of the discomfort were frequently normal, so the recruits were thought to have been "dogging it." When persistent complaints were followed by disability, second X rays taken two weeks later revealed healing fractures.

If you think you may have a stress fracture, I believe it is safe to wait about two weeks before seeking medical evaluation. There are two reasons for this: First, if the ache or pain is minor and not caused by a stress fracture, it may go away in less than a week or two, with proper rest. Second, if you seek medical care before a week or two have passed, an X ray will probably indicate no problem even if you do have a stress fracture. If the pain persists and you return to the doctor several weeks later in frustration, a healing fracture will show up by then in a second X ray.

If you do go to a doctor right away and explain clearly that an increase in activity might have been the cause of pain, the doctor may tell you that you probably have a stress fracture and ask you to return in another week or two for an X ray. This is very sound advice.

While I have said that it is safe to wait two weeks for medical evaluation of a possible stress fracture, I emphatically do not agree with some running books that encourage continued running on a stress fracture. The best way to treat stress fractures is to give them rest from running and jumping. I have seen minor stress fractures become painful complete fractures from ill-advised running on a painful foot. Once a stress fracture has been determined, casting may be necessary to make the foot more comfortable, or simply to protect someone from himself or from an overanxious coach or parent. Again, the best medicine for a stress fracture is rest, even if it must be forced by a cast! Most stress fractures of the foot will heal in four to six weeks if the foot is rested.

Injuries of the Forefoot

A fall from a height or a forced twisting of the foot may result in either a relatively painless or a serious injury. If there is no marked swelling and no bruising, and the individual is able to walk on the foot fairly well, simply apply ice off and on until the swelling is gone. Probably no other treatment will be necessary. However, if the forefoot area is swollen and the pain is so disabling that it is impossible to walk, call a doctor or go to an emergency room.

Between these two extremes, the foot may be painful to walk on and exhibit tenderness and bruising in one localized area (Illustration 2). It is probably fractured, and a doctor should be notified of the fact. You

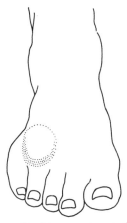

2/Fractured foot. Swelling and bruising anywhere in the forefoot indicates a possible fracture.

may be advised to apply ice for twelve to twenty-four hours and to keep the foot elevated before seeing the doctor. This is not an emergency situation, but you should definitely seek medical attention within a day or so. Treatment for this type of fracture usually consists of wearing a cast or stiff-soled shoe for four to six weeks.

Injury to the Outer Side of the Foot

A common foot injury is a fracture of the base of the fifth metatarsal (Illustration 3). If bruising and tenderness occur only around the bone located in the middle of the outer side of the foot, a fracture is certain. This injury is notorious for slow healing in children and active young adults if not treated in a cast.

The fracture heals slowly because it is a "pull-off" fracture. Every time the foot moves, the peroneus brevis tendon tends to pull the fracture apart, and this delays the healing. A walking cast is certainly very comfortable and, I believe, it is the treatment of choice in any young, active person. Mature sedentary adults do not always need casting.

This type of fracture is not an emergency and can safely be treated with ice and elevation for twenty-four to forty-eight hours, until it is convenient for a doctor to evaluate the problem. But it is imperative

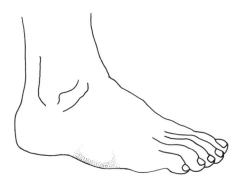

3/Fracture of a fifth metatarsal. If a foot exhibits bruising, swelling, and tenderness along the side, in the area shaded, it is probably fractured.

that medical treatment be obtained within a few days; although many of these fractures may heal by themselves, a significant number will not heal, even after months of inactivity, and can be painfully disabling unless treated properly.

Arch Strain or Pain of the Bottom of the Foot

Pain in the arch or along the bottom of the foot can occur as the result of a sudden injury, such as an uncontrolled jump or hard landing, or from repetitive jumping on a hard surface. It is a rare occurrence in youngsters under twelve, but a common complaint in people over the age of twenty-five, especially if they have changed the surface on which they play tennis or jog, or if they have changed their shoes or worn them down.

If a specific injury is responsible and no swelling or bruising is noted, the plantar fascia, the ligament that supports the arch, is mildly strained. Frequently, ice packs and adequate taping of the arch are all the treatment necessary. An easy solution is to bind a good, soft, commercial arch support to the foot with adhesive tape. If that fails to solve the problem or the pain is disabling, medical evaluation is necessary.

If there was no specific jolt to the foot, the pain almost certainly stems from inflammation of the plantar fascia due to overuse of the foot and arch from too much running or jumping. Or X rays may reveal a heel spur, a calcium deposit on the bottom of the heel where the ligament attaches to the heel. In both cases, inflammation is the problem and treatment is the same. Apply ice and use a heel cup (a soft plastic pressure-relieving cup available in some drug stores) or a soft, flat, doughnut-shaped cushion commercially made for the purpose. For a jogger, properly cushioned shoes with a slightly raised heel may prevent or adequately treat the problem if the pain only occurs when running. However, if the pain becomes severe and disabling, medication or even a cortisone injection may be recommended by your physician. In adults, this condition can be very difficult to treat, and, as a last resort, may require surgery. Surgery will reduce the pain significantly, but may not eliminate it entirely.

Heel Pain

Heel pain and pain where the Achilles tendon attaches to the bone are very common in active, growing children. The weakest areas of any bone in a child are the growth zones, and the more rapidly a child grows, the weaker these areas become. The growth zone for the heel is on the end, as seen in Illustration 4. The Achilles tendon attaches the heel to the three calf muscles, or triceps surae. Thus these three

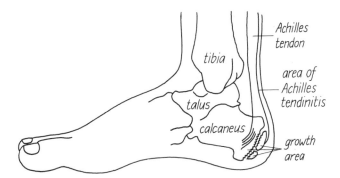

4/A child's heel. In an X ray, the growth zone of the calcaneus, or heel bone, in a child's foot sometimes shows fragmentation. This is not unusual in the heel of a growing child, a common area of minor pain in the young.

powerful calf muscles, indirectly through the tendon, pull on a weak area of a child's bone, which is also subjected to pounding on hard surfaces such as paved playgrounds. In a sense, any ensuing discomfort is a growing pain, but it is also an overuse pain, and functions as a warning that it's time to slow down. This problem seems to have become more common as more playgrounds have been paved.

If there is no swelling and only some mild to moderate tenderness in the area, ask the child two questions: "When does it hurt?" and "Does it ever stop you from playing?" If it only hurts after running or jumping and does not prevent the child from participating in an activity, then you can safely treat the soreness with ice. When the child is not playing it will help to insert a quarter-inch-thick felt pad in the heel of his or her sneaker or shoe to raise the heel. Likewise, high-heeled cowboy boots may be more comfortable for a time. If these measures fail, consult your physician.

When I see a child who comes home every night after baseball, football, or basketball practice and invariably complains about a sore heel, I will usually give him two options: Either he stops playing, to see if the heel continues to hurt. Or, if play must go on, no more complaining is allowed and he must ice down his own heels. Your child should not at the same time have both the right to complain and the right to play. This treatment is very effective for mild cases. If the pain is constant, however, or if it prevents the child from participating in any activities or is present in the morning when the child first gets up, medical consultation is necessary.

Sprained Ankles

Sprained ankles are rare in children under the age of twelve. Their ligaments are simply stronger than their bones, so a bone will usually give first. The weakest parts of any child's bone are the growth zones at each end, and the more rapidly a child grows, the weaker these zones become. Therefore, assume that any injury in a child that is accompanied by swelling and bruising around a joint is a fracture until proved otherwise by an expert.

In children over the age of twelve, on the other hand, ankle sprains are one of the most common injuries. Treatment depends on three factors: (1) the severity of the sprain; (2) the amount of pain; and (3) the age of the patient.

Generally, the better the athlete, the more intensively the sprain should be treated, because the demands on the ankles of an active adolescent are rigorous. For stability, the ankle joint depends upon ligaments and a solid fit between the bones. If the ligaments are torn and do not heal tightly, then a so-called weak or trick ankle will result, leading to repeated bouts of giving way, instability, and easy re-spraining of the ankle. Therefore only the mildest of sprains will require no treatment in young athletes. Severe sprains almost certainly need casting, and, in rare circumstances, surgery may be required. In contrast, even severe sprains in the sedentary adult can sometimes be treated with an elastic bandage and neglect.

The difference between a mild sprain and a severe sprain has to do with the number of ligaments injured and which ones they are. In a

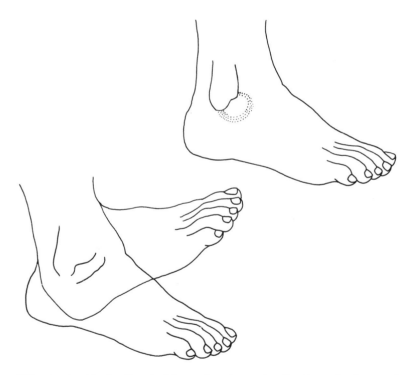

5/Sprained ankle. Swelling, bruising, and tenderness localized immediately around the front of the anklebone *(top)* are signs of a simple sprain. An ability to move the foot up and down four or five inches with relatively little pain also indicates a simple sprain *(bottom)*.

mildly sprained ankle, the pain is only moderate, and the athlete should be able to move the foot up or down at the ankle with little or no additional pain (see Illustration 5). Most importantly, tenderness and bruising should be localized in the area immediately around the front of the ankle bone. Apply ice, tape the ankle, and give it a few days' rest.

(For an easy way to tape an ankle, run three or four long half-inch-wide strips of adhesive tape, overlapping the edges, from about two inches above the outside ankle bone, down under the foot and up the inside of the leg to the level at which you started. Next, add four to six overlapping strips of tape, across the front of the ankle; cross over the vertical strips of tape but do not go beyond them. This will leave the back of the ankle free for adequate circulation.)

An athlete with a mild sprain should be able to walk with only minimal discomfort. If a sporting activity is important to the individual, it can be resumed, as long as the ankle is taped as just described. With proper care, any tenderness should be gone in ten to twenty-one days, and the athlete should experience complete recovery.

In a severe sprain more than one ankle ligament is injured (Illustrations 6 and 7) and there is swelling, bruising, and, frequently, tenderness on both sides of the ankle. The inner side of the ankle is rarely injured in a mild sprain. Marked swelling or pain in or around the ankle should be considered signs of a severe sprain, at least. Likewise, if the

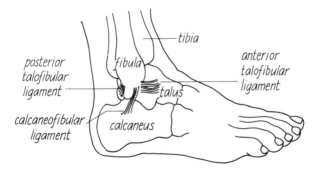

6/Ankle ligaments susceptible to injury. Any ankle sprain affects the anterior talofibular ligament. If the sprain is simple, the ligament is partially torn. The calcaneofibular ligament is an important stabilizer of the ankle; if it is injured, the result is a severe ankle sprain. Injury to the posterior talofibular ligament, another stabilizer, is also severe.

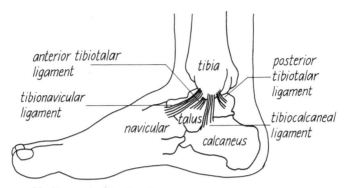

7/Inner ankle ligaments. The four ligaments at the inner ankle comprise what is called the deltoid ligament, the main stabilizer of the ankle. A severe ankle sprain results from an injury to this area.

athlete is unable to walk on the ankle or move the foot up or down at the ankle joint, a severe sprain (if not a fracture) is indicated.

Even an orthopedic surgeon may have difficulty telling the difference between a severe sprain and a fractured ankle without X rays, so a severe sprain deserves to be seen by a physician. A permanently weak ankle may result from failure to adequately treat these ligaments. If the athlete is comfortable, the application of ice packs and elevation of the foot for twenty-four to thirty-six hours overnight are safe temporary treatments.

There are some exceptions to waiting overnight, however. The following sitations demand emergency treatment: If there is tenderness of the fibula bone that runs along the outside of the ankle or leg (Illustration 6), consider the ankle to be fractured and seek emergency medical care. Any deformity, an open wound, severe pain, poor circulation, or numbness of the foot also requires emergency medical attention. Lack of treatment could be disastrous.

First aid for a severe ankle injury consists of the application of a splint and ice, and elevation of the ankle. A splint can be improvised out of rolled-up newspapers or a piece of cardboard. If available, inflatable air splints are excellent, and a pillow of some kind will help to raise the foot. Loosely attach the splint with strips of cloth or tape. If the ankle is deformed and you must handle the situation alone, do not, in any way, try to correct the deformity. Even if a bone is sticking out of the skin, do not attempt to return it to a normal position. Unless it is surgically cleaned, putting a dirty or contaminated bone back into a wound greatly increases the risk of infection and may result in the loss of a leg, or death. If the injured person has an open wound, simply cover it with the cleanest material available. Then, with two hands, gently lift the injured foot and ankle onto a splint, board, or pillow and gently support them the best way possible, without tying in any way, while getting the patient to an emergency room. *Caution:* It is better to wait ten or fifteen minutes for a paramedic or ski patrol than to improperly splint and move a person with a severly injured ankle by yourself.

Weak Ankles

Many athletes are troubled by "weak" ankles. This usually means their ankles will either give out frequently on uneven ground or will sprain with relatively minor twists. The most common causes of this problem are inadequately treated ankle sprains and poor healing of severe ankle sprains.

If you are troubled with a weak ankle, there are two things to do. Tape the ankle for support every time you exercise or play on it and wear sport shoes with a flared heel if you can play in them. The flared heel tends to prevent twisting and will help stabilize the ankle, even for walking.

If you are still unable to play in spite of these measures, the ankle should be evaluated by an orthopedic surgeon. For severe disability and gross weakness of the ankle ligaments, surgery may be beneficial. In rare cases, a weak ankle is caused by a bone chip in the ankle joint that must be removed by surgery.

Taping of Ankles

There is some difference of opinion about the value of taping a normal ankle. I believe taping will help prevent many ankle sprains in those sports that have a high incidence of ankle injuries, especially football and basketball at the high school level and beyond. Most authorities agree that taping is valuable, and we all agree that it is of benefit to the injured or weak ankle.

10 / Legs

F OR safety's sake, let's begin with a proviso. When a leg is obviously fractured, or it is clear that the leg is badly hurt and severely painful, it is best to splint or immobilize the injured limb in the position you find it. Do not pull on it; simply transport the injured person immediately to an emergency room.

Muscle Cramps

Ordinary muscle cramps in the legs may result from a variety of things. Salt depletion from excessive sweating or running in high heat and humidity is one. Other possible causes include overfatigue, too tight taping or binding (such as by the cuff of a uniform around the calf), sudden changes in temperature (chilling or sudden overheating), and failure to warm up properly.

Treatment of ordinary muscle cramps starts with the obvious: First try to eliminate the cause. Then try a gentle massage of the calf. If a cramp is severe and the athlete is writhing and clutching a calf in agony, try this basic remedy: Gently grasp the foot of the cramped leg and push against it while the athlete pushes against you (Illustration 8).

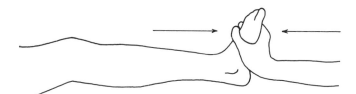

8/Emergency treatment for a muscle cramp

Pushing the foot against any solid object will also work, if you are alone. This will usually bring dramatic relief. If there is no further pain, swelling, tenderness, or limping after a few minutes, it is probably safe to resume the athletic endeavor. If, however, there is tenderness and pain, it is better to rest, ice the muscle down, and eliminate any running or jumping for as long as the tenderness persists. Deep, vigorous massage is definitely not recommended.

"Charley horse" is the common name for a severe muscle cramp that often comes on suddenly and painfully from no known cause. It may be the result of overstretching a muscle or tendon group, which can lead to severe spasms. Another cause could be a slight tear in the muscle. If the pain stems from anything more than a slight muscle tear, it will not go away quickly, and rest and ice are clearly warranted. If the pain persists and is disabling, especially if it lasts more than twenty-four hours, a physician should be consulted.

Achilles Tendinitis

Pain in the Achilles tendon is common in all age groups. The tendon is the largest in the body and connects the powerful calf muscles to the heel. You cannot take a step, run, or jump without using the Achilles tendons.

The most common cause of Achilles tendinitis is overuse of these tendons by too much running or jumping, especially on hard surfaces. The other cause is a sudden, unexpected stretching of the tendon. Both result in pain, probably from microscopic tears in the tendon. The body's attempt to heal these injuries results in inflammation and pain.

The first treatment, prevention, should be obvious. Don't abuse or overuse your body. If you experience mild pain, a heel lift is the best treatment: Insert a quarter-inch to half-inch felt pad in the heel of your shoe. Commercially made pads are available and may be doubled if necessary. Shoes with slightly raised heels can also help. Ice is again the drug of choice and should be applied before and after activity, though rest is the best cure. Such tendinitis may take ten to twenty-one days to disappear. To avoid the development of a chronic case, do not rush the recuperative time. All pain should be absent before activity is resumed.

Achilles Tendon Ruptures

There are two types of Achilles tendon rupture. One occurs in the young adult from a strong, forceful contraction of the muscle, so strong, in fact, that it pulls the tendon in half. The other is found in the middle-aged athlete and is probably the result of a less violent pull on an abnormally weak tendon. In both cases, medical attention is mandatory.

Typically, a sudden move will be made on the leg, and a severe, sharp pain will be felt in the calf. The athlete almost always mistakenly believes that someone kicked or shot him in the calf. This is usually followed by some disability and a sense of weakness in that area. These symptoms should be medically evaluated. Once the tendon is ruptured it can be deceptively painless.

A ruptured tendon usually calls for surgical repair. If treatment is delayed for more than ten to fourteen days a good result is less likely than if medical attention is sought within the first week. Recovery from an operation on a ruptured tendon usually requires six to eight weeks in a cast and four to six months of relative inactivity.

Shin Splints

"Shin splints" is the lay term for pain along the front of the leg between the knee and ankle where the muscles that move the foot and ankle attach to the tibia (shinbone). As a result of inadequate training, fatigue, or poor coordination, these muscles sometimes have a tendency to tear away slightly from the bone, causing pain and inflammation. If the pain is mild, then rest and ice are the treatments of choice. Taping the front half of the leg with horizontal, overlapping strips of tape may make the leg more comfortable during an activity. These mild shin splints can sometimes be prevented by avoiding hard surfaces when running, warming up adequately before sprinting, and by using good running technique.

The cause of shin splints is still poorly understood, and, although many people voice strong opinions about it and the proper treatment to use, no one knows for sure why the condition is so painful and troublesome.

If the pain at the front of the leg is more than a nuisance and persists for more than two weeks, you may have a stress fracture of either the tibia or the fibula, or of both. During those first two weeks, the condition may be easily misdiagnosed because stress fractures do not show up on an X ray for about fourteen days. Even if you think you have shin splints, you would do well to read the following section on stress fractures.

A rare case of shin splints that occurs in both athletes and nonathletes is manifested by pain over the outer front side of the leg in the region of the muscles. Every time the stricken person either walks fast or starts to run, the pain begins. As the walking or running becomes more rapid, the pain grows increasingly severe, and does not go away. If strong pain is experienced at the front of the leg during vigorous activity and does not go away after fifteen minutes' rest, an immediate visit to a physician or an emergency room is mandatory.

Rapid emergency care is recommended because constant, severe pain that endures for more than fifteen to thirty minutes may be caused by marked swelling of the muscles. Muscles are surrounded by bone and strong tissues, which form a tight compartment. If the muscles swell up for some reason, they may block circulation in the leg and cause considerable pain. If such pain is ignored for hours, permanent weakness and muscle death can result. The medical term for this condition is anterior compartment syndrome.

Diagnosis in mild cases of this condition is very difficult without an appropriate history. But if such a pain occurs every time you walk a certain distance, or especially when you run—regardless of the amount of training or rest preceding the exertion—your doctor may suspect anterior compartment syndrome. Because a clear, definite history is most helpful in evaluating the problem, keep a record of when the pain comes and goes and review it carefully with your physician.

Another way to help diagnose this condition is to determine whether you can feel the pulse on the top of your foot (some people do not have a pulse on the top of their feet). Feel the pulse on your foot prior to exercising. If you feel a pulse before but cannot feel it again after the exercise, when the pain occurs, then you almost certainly have anterior compartment syndrome and the only beneficial treatment for it must be made by an orthopedic surgeon. The surgery for this condition is relatively simple, and recovery takes only a few weeks. Normal function is usually restored, but a slight bulge in the muscle may remain.

Another type of shin splint sometimes occurs to people with low arches. For a discussion of this problem see page 62.

Stress Fractures

Bone is living tissue that is constantly being made, changed, and destroyed, all at the same time. And it is not a solid structure. Thus, if a repetitive load, such as in running, is placed on the bones of the foot, leg, or thigh, and it exceeds the strength of the bone, the bone will fail and a stress, or fatigue, fracture will be the result (Illustration 9).

A stress fracture can occur in a world-class runner, but it is much more common in the novice or unconditioned runner who tries to get back in shape too quickly or runs too far too fast too soon. Among students, stress fractures are far more common in the autumn than at any other time of year because regular training is not usually kept up during the summer. A student who tries to rush getting in shape may develop leg pain after two to three weeks of running.

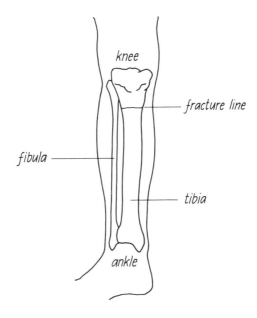

9/A stress fracture. Two weeks after an injury, a clear stress fracture may turn up in an X ray. If the injury is less than two weeks old, any X rays could appear normal, even if the fracture is present.

If a doctor is consulted and X rays are taken less than two weeks after the onset of pain, the X rays will be normal, the patient will be told that it is probably shin splints, and the pain will persist. Pain that lasts more than two weeks usually indicates a stress fracture, which, by then, will show up on an X ray. This means four to six weeks more of enforced rest, the best medication possible, and perhaps a cast. At that point, start activity slowly and stop again if any pain recurs.

Running on a stress fracture risks more serious damage to the bone. It can fracture completely, requiring the standard orthopedic care — which for the tibia of a young adult may be as long as six months. Thus, it is extremely unwise to run on a stress fracture.

As a parent, what do you do? If your child begins to complain of shin splints and finds that he or she is unable to run or jump because of pain, any sporting activity should be stopped or reduced drastically right away. In my view, decreased activity within pain tolerance is reasonable, but if the pain persists for two weeks, it is a good idea to seek medical care and have X rays taken.

When you do seek medical care, it is very important to tell a doctor the whole story, especially if it concerns any increased running. On an X ray, a healing stress fracture can resemble an early stage in a malignant bone tumor. Therefore, if you have only mentioned leg pain in a general way, the doctor may recommend a biopsy. The diagnosis of a stress fracture should be obvious to any orthopedic surgeon who has been given an adequate history.

Fracture of the Fibula

When pain develops after a blow to the outside of the leg, the fibula may be fractured, even if there is no deformity. If the injured person is relatively comfortable walking and only feels pain when running, it is perfectly safe to apply ice packs to the leg and rest for a day or two. Persistent pain after that stage requires a physician's care, and X rays will be used to make a diagnosis. A fracture from a blow is usually easy to read on an X ray. Treatment, as for a stress fracture, will depend upon the fracture and may require casting.

Bruises

In sports that may involve kicking, a player is liable to get very nasty bruises along the front edge of the tibia. At times these bruises look quite ugly and can be very colorful, perhaps a combination of blue, green, and yellow, depending upon how recent they are. If absolutely no pain is felt when the athlete is walking, jumping, or running, then ice packs should be applied. Although it may take two to three weeks for these bruises to go away and they may look horrible, they are usually of no medical consequence.

Bruises accompanied by an inability to walk or run on the leg or to move the foot should be medically treated within twenty-four hours. Seek emergency medical attention·if the swelling begins to increase or severe pain develops.

11 / Knees

MANY athletes and parents fear knee injuries more than any other kind because they are the most common causes of permanent disability in sports. Injuries to this vital joint are increasing in frequency and severity because people are growing bigger and the improved traction of artificial surfaces tends to hold the foot in place, thereby increasing the risk of harm to the leg.

Yet the general public's understanding of the knee joint is rather poor. In fact, lay terms regarding some key structures of the knee are quite misleading and the opposite of what anatomists use. Therefore, to better understand the knee and the injuries that plague it, we should first review some basic anatomy and biomechanics.

Structure of the Knee

Many people think of the knee joint in terms of a simple hinge, but it is far more complex than that. It is true that the knee bends, but in doing so, it also glides, slides, and rotates. It is actually an unstable joint and depends on soft tissue structures (muscles, tendons, ligaments, and cartilage) for its stability.

The upper surface of the tibia (or shinbone) is a flat, plateaulike structure with two bony spikes in the middle, and the lower end of the femur, or thigh bone, which meets it, forms two semicircular "knuckles" (Illustrations 10 and 11). One can easily see that these bony configurations have no more inherent stability than a beginner on roller skates. Thus, the soft tissue structures surrounding the joint are vital to its stability.

In front of the knee joint are the quadriceps muscle, the patella (kneecap), and the patellar tendon. The kneecap, known as a sesamoid bone to anatomists, actually lies between the tendons that connect the tibia with the quadriceps (four-part) muscle. This muscle at the front of the thigh is the most powerful one in the body and is used to straighten out the knee.

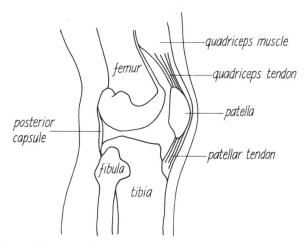

10/Side view of important knee anatomy

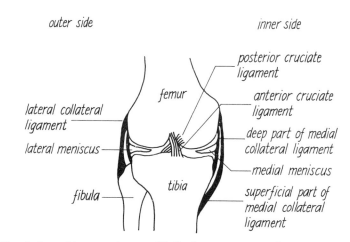

11/Front view of knee anatomy, with the kneecap removed

The kneecap serves two functions: In a kneeling position it is a firm, thick, bony barrier that protects the knee joint against foreign objects. Its second function is as a lever to increase the power of the quadriceps muscle in straightening the knee. Although the kneecap lies in a shallow groove formed by the "knuckles" along the front of the femur, it is held in place by relatively weak tissues and is vulnerable to dislocations that may occur with relatively minor trauma.

The undersurface of the kneecap is considered a part of the knee joint itself. It is covered with smooth, glistening cartilage whose normal appearance is white, firm, and very smooth. The cartilage, which is supplied with tiny nerves, is quite sensitive, as are the nerves supplying the bone under the cartilage. This is why self-defense courses teach blows to the kneecap.

On three sides of the knee joint a strong ligament or complex of ligaments holds the bones together and provides stability. The back of the joint is supported by an extremely powerful group of ligaments called the posterior capsule (Illustration 10). The outer side of the joint is held by the lateral collateral ligament, while the inner side is reinforced by two ligaments, one superficial and the other deep, known together as the medial collateral ligament (Illustration 11).

Inside the knee joint there are four equally important stabilizing structures. Two are the main ligaments within the joint, the crossing

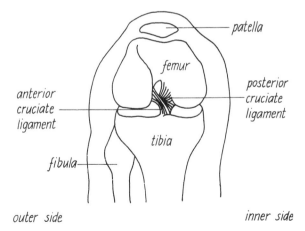

12/Front view of the knee, bent 90° to show the cruciate ligament inside the knee joint

or cruciate ligaments (Illustration 12). The anterior cruciate ligament is extremely strong and its main function is to prevent a forward shift of the knee joint; the posterior cruciate ligament prevents a backward shift of the joint. The other two structures of note within the knee are commonly called cartilage because they are made of specialized fibro-cartilage. The correct anatomic term for them, however, is menisci. The medial meniscus fits into the inner side of the knee joint, the lateral meniscus is between the outer sides (Illustration 13). They are further distinguished by shape: the lateral meniscus is almost circular, while the medial meniscus is like a large *C*. Although they are not completely understood, it is obvious from their location, shape, and consistency that the menisci serve at least three functions: First, they cup the knee joint so that, in a sense, they provide runners on which the femur can glide securely over the tibial plateaus. Second, the menisci are spacers

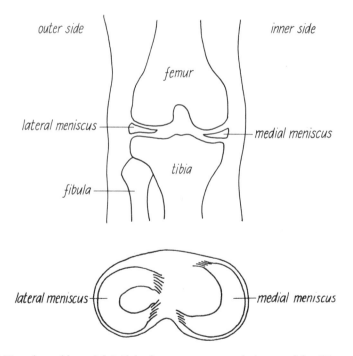

13/Top view of knee joint. If the femur were removed, the top of the tibia would be shaped something like a peanut with a crescent-shaped piece of cartilage, or meniscus, at each end. Note the difference in shape between the menisci.

that fill the gaps on the outer sides of the knee and thus help to support it. Third, they serve, to a minor degree, as shock absorbers.

The entire top surface of the tibia, the lower end of the femur, and the undersurface of the patella or kneecap are covered with a smooth, white, glistening cartilage called articular (joint surface) cartilage. (This should not be confused with the specialized cartilage of the menisci.)

Finally, the entire knee joint is lubricated by a clear yellow liquid called synovial (joint) fluid. Normally the knee produces approximately two quarts of this material a day, but much of it is absorbed, so the full amount is never there at any one time.

Pain and Noise Under the Kneecap

The most common type of mild, or even moderate to severe, knee pain with no special history of injury occurs along the underside of the kneecap. The question that arises is how to evaluate such continuing pain when there is no evidence of swelling.

First, see if the knee hurts when going up and down stairs, kneeling, or when getting out of a deep, overstuffed chair. Then find out if it makes a creaking noise, or if the person feels a crunchy sensation, or if, at times, the knee pops so loudly that other people can hear it. The next step is to put your hand on the kneecap and, with the person sitting, ask him or her to bend and straighten the knee. If you feel a sandpaper-type effect or hear or feel a grating in the area that hurts, the condition is almost certainly what is called chondromalacia of the patella. That imposing-sounding term means nothing more than a softening of the undersurface (the joint surface) of the kneecap.

There is little reason to worry or seek medical attention for this condition if the person experiences only minimal pain that does not limit participation in sports, or if the knee only hurts occasionally when the person walks up or down stairs or kneels. *Caution:* If there is swelling, medical evaluation is recommended; never ignore a swollen knee.

If a child is suffering from such pain in the knee when he or she participates in gym and is not eager to continue the activity, then limit the offending activity until the symptoms are no longer disabling. A note from a doctor will probably be required because most physical education teachers are not sympathetic to this problem, believing that the student is just seeking an excuse to get out of gym. If the pain is moderate to severe, it will probably have to be evaluated medically.

The exact cause of most cases of chondromalacia is unknown, but this kind of softening or roughening of the undersurface of the kneecap can result from a blow or a fall on the kneecap that drives it into the end of the femur bone. It can also result from repeated dislocations of the kneecap.

In my opinion, chondromalacia is the single most frustrating condition to treat in all of orthopedics. There is little doubt that increasing the strength of the thigh muscles, especially the quadriceps muscle, is an important way of decreasing the pain of chondromalacia. The unfortunate and frustrating part is that the exercises needed to increase strength frequently aggravate the pain. Thus, in some respects, the cure can be worse than the problem.

Isometric exercises are recommended for chondromalacia. They can tighten up the quadriceps muscle while the knee is kept straight. Some people recommend that the foot be turned in slightly while exercising to strengthen the inner muscles of the thigh as well.

Here is one such exercise for the thigh muscles. Start in a sitting position. Lift the leg and hold it out straight in front of you for 10 seconds before lowering it. Repeat 10 times, holding a full 10 seconds each time. After several days, when that becomes easy, tie a one-pound weight to your leg and repeat the same exercise. (Graduated weights are available in sporting goods stores.) As the leg gets stronger, the weight on it can gradually be increased a pound at a time. Good average strength is about 10 pounds of lift, 20 pounds is very good.

If the knee can tolerate movement, it may be beneficial to do exercises that require bending and straightening it, especially if the foot is turned in slightly as the leg is moved. Here is a bending exercise. Again, start in a sitting position. Lift the leg in front of you and then bend and straighten the knee 10 times. Do three sets of 10 bends each. The leg can be strengthened gradually and comfortably by adding weight to it over a period of weeks. The average person should do this exercise once a day, the athlete twice. Performing the same bending exercise while lying face down would also be beneficial. The strength of the leg can be used to determine the type of activity you are fit to perform. If you can only lift ten pounds or less, you probably need crutches or a cast; at twenty pounds it is safe to run or jog in a straight line; at thirty pounds you can participate in most non-collision sports; and at fifty pounds unrestricted sporting activity is permissible.

Occasionally a doctor may recommend medicine to decrease the irritation inside the knee, but medication is often of no help whatsoever.

If the pain remains severe and disabling and exercise, rest, and medication have all failed, surgery may be recommended. In one type of knee surgery the rough area of cartilage on the underside of the kneecap is surgically shaved smooth or, if necessary, is removed down to the bone in the hope that smooth cartilage will grow back. This operation is successful only 60 percent of the time. If shaving fails to provide relief, then removal of the kneecap may be indicated. This obviously is the final step in treatment and should be done only when all else has failed. The operation has a 90 percent probability of success, but it weakens the knee.

If you have chondromalacia, the worst sports for it are ones that provide excessive stress on the knee. Jumping leads, followed by basketball and volleyball, though occasionally runners suffer from chondromalacia as well.

It was once thought that chondromalacia would lead to the accelerated development of arthritis on the undersurface of the kneecap, in the joint between the kneecap and the femur (thighbone). Recent studies have suggested that while there is some increased risk of arthritis in this area, even moderately severe chondromalacia does not necessarily become arthritic. This supports the argument that if the symptoms of chondromalacia can be ignored without excessive discomfort, it is probably safe to do so.

Kneecap Dislocation

If someone occasionally complains of a kneecap that pops in and out of place but the person can walk and run normally and there is no swelling, then medical attention is probably unnecessary. If the kneecap continues to slip "in and out of place," or it becomes dislocated (Illustration 14) and locks, causing extreme pain, or there is continual or recurring swelling in the knee, medical attention is necessary. Marked swelling of the knee is reason enough to go to an emergency room, as is a kneecap that remains dislocated.

When an orthopedic examination reveals no problem other than a kneecap that slips partially or completely out of place, some hard decisions are necessary. Surgery is the only effective means of preventing further recurrences of such kneecap dislocations. If the symptoms are only mild to moderate and the offending activity can be discontinued, surgery is certainly not mandatory. Try the exercises outlined in the previous section to strengthen

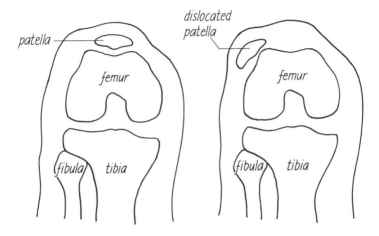

14/Front view of the knee, bent at a 45° angle. A dislocated patella is sometimes mistakenly called a dislocated knee. It causes severe pain and disability. The patella (kneecap) normally sits in a groove at the center of the femur (left). Sometimes it will start to slip out of place without dislocating completely. A partially dislocated (subluxed) patella is accompanied by a sensation of giving way, or starting to go out of place, and, at times, pain, but it always slips back.

the thigh muscles and decrease the symptoms. But if the injury is disabling, surgery may be the best choice.

You should also know that every time the kneecap dislocates, the back of it may receive some damage that could lead to the development of chondromalacia. A dislocating patella is actually one of the main causes of chondromalacia.

Growing Pains (Osgood-Schlatter's Disease)

The most common cause of knee pain in adolescents is Osgood-Schlatter's disease. The problem is found only in rapidly growing teenagers and it is probably the easiest condition in orthopedics to diagnose. If the pain is localized in the area where the patellar tendon connects the kneecap to the shinbone, and if any swelling or marked tenderness appears only in that area, the teenager probably has Osgood-Schlatter's disease (Illustration 15).

When the powerful quadriceps muscle in the thigh pulls on a growth zone in the leg, it can lead to Osgood-Schlatter's disease. The quad-

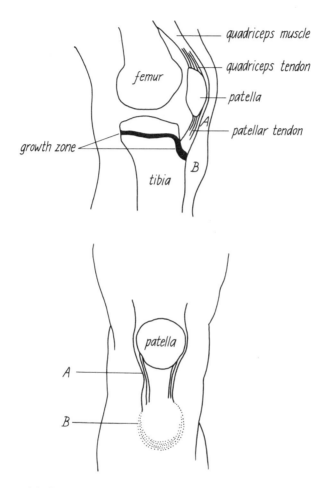

15/Areas of the knee affected by jumper's knee and Osgood-Schlatter's disease.
Tenderness a little to the side and just beneath the kneecap, in area A, is usually
associated with jumper's knee, a condition that can occur in an athlete of any age who
does an excessive amount of jumping. Swelling and tenderness about an inch below
the kneecap, in area B, are typical of Osgood-Schlatter's disease, a malady that occurs
only in rapidly growing, active adolescents.

riceps muscle, actually a group of four muscles on the front of the
thigh, pulls through the kneecap to straighten out the knee. The muscle
is attached by a strong tendon to a growth zone, or apophysis, in the

shinbone. In rapidly growing children this growth zone is the weakest area of the bone, so when the strongest muscle in the body pulls against it, the result is often inflammation and pain. In a sense it's a true growth pain, that can occur in one or both knees.

Osgood-Schlatter's disease is self-remedying. It goes away completely when growth ceases. In girls this usually happens at age fourteen or fifteen, in boys somewhere between the ages of sixteen and eighteen.

While mild cases require no medical treatment, they do need much understanding. The typical patient with Osgood-Schlatter's is an extremely active young athlete who may play basketball, baseball, or volleyball, or do gymnastics for a whole afternoon, without having significant pain. Afterward he or she will complain about painful knees. This can precipitate a family battle, in which the parents tell their child to quit sports and the adolescent vehemently refuses to do so. This frustrating situation usually continues until medical advice is sought. The doctor makes a diagnosis of Osgood-Schlatter's disease, and tells the athlete to stop playing all sports for a period of time. Casting may even be recommended.

This may precipitate another family crisis, with the adolescent refusing treatment or, worse yet for the pocketbook, destroying the cast. Parents then get aggravated at the amount of money they are spending for treatment, which causes continued deterioration of the parent-child relationship.

If your child has Osgood-Schlatter's first encourage him or her to participate in sports that don't require a great deal of jumping or running. Second, insist that knee pads be worn—slightly below the knees—for protection in sports like basketball, volleyball, and gymnastics. Kneeling should also be avoided because it is quite painful. If the child insists on running or jumping, apply ice to the area after the activity. Last, reassure the child that the condition will eventually go away, but it will last as long as vigorous activity persists and rapid growth continues.

My usual treatment for mild cases is a long talk with both adolescent and parent. I will tell the child that he (or she) can have one of two things: either continued sports without interference from parent or doctor, or the right to complain about knee pain, but no sports. The child may not have both. This solves the problem in 95 percent of the mild cases of Osgood-Schlatter's disease.

Children who have pain that limits their ability to play, or feel pain when they are climbing stairs or walking, have moderate to severe cases of the disease. When the pain is that strong, medical attention is warranted. This may include X rays, casting, and medications. Some parents may ask for cortisone shots for their children, but I am not in favor of this because I believe rest is the best cure. (See the section on cortisone.) I also believe that pain protects a child from too much activity. To mask it artificially risks serious damage to the growth zone at the knee.

One possible complication of Osgood-Schlatter's disease is the development of a bone fragment in the tendon between the kneecap and the shinbone (Illustration 16). This free bone fragment frequently accounts for the knobby knee seen in Osgood-Schlatter's. The presence of such a fragment always makes kneeling a somewhat painful proposition, and, if the presence of the fragment is painful after the child stops growing, the only effective treatment is surgery.

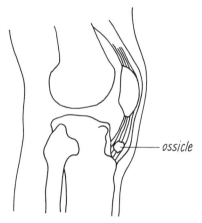

ossicle

16/Osgood-Schlatter's disease with an ossicle. Sometimes an ossicle (bone fragment) develops in the tendon of an adolescent who is experiencing growing pains. It causes a knobby-knee appearance and pain when kneeling.

Jumper's Knee

As its name implies, jumper's knee is an affliction that results from excessive jumping. It occurs most commonly in basketball and volleyball players of all ages, and it seems to be on the rise, perhaps because those sports are becoming year-round activities and because more sports are being played on hard surfaces.

The diagnosis of jumper's knee is very easy to make. It is characterized by pain—occurring during or after jumping—where the kneecap attaches to the patellar tendon (Illustration 15). Jumper's knee is thought to be caused by small tears where the tendon attaches to the kneecap. The tears fail to heal and then become inflamed.

The best treatment is prevention. This includes proper strengthening exercises for quadriceps, hamstring, and calf muscles as well as proper warming up prior to vigorous jumping. In addition, training should be planned to avoid overuse and abuse of the knee in repetitive jumping. A properly cushioned shoe and the avoidance of jumping on extremely hard surfaces are also recommended.

If the pain is only mild, then rest from repetitive jumping, plus ice and possibly aspirin, should be prescribed. If the pain is beyond response to these treatments, however, medical help is needed. Jumper's knee is a difficult condition to treat if it fails to respond to simple conservative measures. Prolonged rest, even in a cast, may be necessary. Should this fail in severe cases, then surgery may be the only solution.

Torn Cartilage

The knee, as we have seen, has two special pieces of cartilage called menisci, located between the thigh- and shinbones. The injury of a meniscus requires a rotation or twisting stress on the knee. When someone has a foot planted on the ground and twists, pivots, or is tackled so that a meniscus is pinched between the two bones, the meniscus can tear in one of several ways (Illustration 17).

If your meniscus tears you may feel an acute pain or a sudden giving way, or you will hear a pop, or actually collapse to the ground feeling that the knee became dislocated. Usually it is possible to get up afterward and walk around. You may even be able to run and resume activity again. But once a cartilage has been torn in this way, the knee will continue to give or pop out whenever the same kind of rotation stress is applied to the affected meniscus. Sometimes the symptoms can go away for long periods of time, even years, only to recur with a sudden twist or a wrong step on the leg.

Most people who have a torn meniscus are unable to resume activity with the same confidence that preceded the injury. The knee may

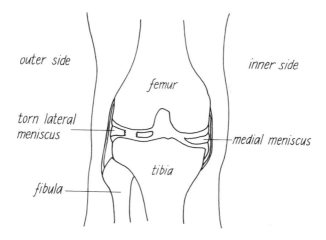

outer side

inner side

femur

torn lateral
meniscus

medial meniscus

tibia

fibula

17/Front view of the knee, with a completely torn lateral meniscus

swell the first time it is injured, but often there will be little or no
swelling. If the meniscus pops back into place, the athlete can simply
get up and seem fine for long periods of time. A torn meniscus is not
a life- or limb-threatening emergency, and unless the pain is acute and
severe or the knee has marked swelling, there is really no reason to
visit an emergency room. A consultation with a physician or an orthopedic surgeon within a reasonable period of time is the best check.

The recurrent popping and giving out of a torn meniscus will probably cause a small amount of damage to the joint surface every time
it happens. Over a period of years this giving way and popping back
and forth will definitely lead to an early wear-and-tear degenerative
type of arthritis in the joint.

The problem is further complicated because some orthopedic surgeons feel that removal of the meniscus leads to an increased rate of
wear and tear in the knee after surgery. This is a moot point, however,
since the knee is already damaged and there is little question that
trauma to any knee accelerates the development of arthritis. A badly
torn meniscus left in place can eventually do severe damage to a knee.

Reasons for seeking orthopedic consultation for a torn meniscus
include recurring disability, insecurity on the knee, and the inability to
resume activity. There is also the hope that surgery may prevent the
development of arthritis of the knee from the recurrent giving way.

The treatment for a torn meniscus is its removal. Once it is gone, if there are no other abnormalities within the joint, the mechanical problem of the knee's giving way and popping should be solved. The loss of a meniscus can usually be compensated for by intensive strengthening of both the quadriceps and hamstring muscles. If the surgery went well and the athlete does exercises faithfully, a return to full participation without any restrictions in his or her favorite sport or vocation can be expected. But resumption of sports or activity before strength has returned can lead to further injury to the knee and permanent damage.

If a torn meniscus stays wedged in the knee joint, locking it or blocking motion, it is a semi-emergency situation. Often, but not always, this condition is accompanied by a great deal of pain. Surgery to remove the meniscus should be performed within two weeks because the constant pressure of the meniscus between the two bones can lead to permanent destruction of the joint surface and very early arthritis. If a knee locks and stays that way, seek orthopedic consultation immediately.

Injuries to the Medial Collateral Ligament

Injuries to the medial collateral ligament (the ligament on the inner side of the knee) are classified as mild, moderate, or severe. Mild injuries rarely come to the attention of physicians. Many players won't complain about them to anyone except their trainer or coach. A mild injury consists of a small stretch in the ligament, and the strength of the pain is the only problem. Complete recovery can be expected in a week to ten days. Ice and rest are the treatment of choice. Strengthening exercises may also speed recovery.

Moderate strains or injuries to the medial collateral ligament involve partial tearing and weakening of the ligament. With proper treatment (usually casting or splinting for a period of three to six weeks) full recovery can be expected.

In severe injuries the ligament is completely ruptured (Illustration 18). These ruptures almost always occur when the foot is planted on the ground and the outer side of the knee is hit. In very serious injuries it is easy to see how the medial collateral ligament, the medial meniscus, and possibly the posterior capsule and the anterior and/or posterior cruciate ligaments could also be damaged. The pain ensuing from a rupture of the medial collateral ligament is usually quite severe and disability will be marked. It will feel as though something in the knee has been torn and walking, let alone running, is usually impossible. Cutting, or quick turning, is also impossible. There may be no swelling, because when the knee joint is torn open the blood cannot collect there.

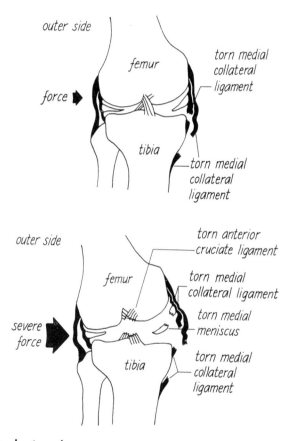

18/Severe and extremely severe sprains of the medial collateral ligament. The term "severe" in regard to a sprain or tear in a medial collateral ligament means that the ligament is torn completely through (top). In a mild to moderate sprain, the ligament is not completely torn.
An injury that involves tears of both the anterior cruciate ligaments and the medial meniscus is very serious and extremely painful (bottom). It almost amounts to a true dislocation of the knee.

Surgery is by far the best treatment for a medial collateral ligament rupture, since it provides the best means of realigning torn ligament ends, permitting them to heal satisfactorily.

Occasionally someone will recover fully without surgery from a serious sporting accident that was diagnosed as severely torn knee ligaments. But this can happen only if the medial collateral ligament alone is torn. Also, the ligament must be torn in the right place and no harm can be done to the meniscus. However, it is virtually impossible to diagnose these tears, and that type of uncomplicated injury is the exception rather than the rule. To defer surgery on an outside chance like that is similar to playing Russian roulette: the odds are against you.

If injury is limited to the medial collateral ligament, the results of surgery are usually quite favorable and most activities can be resumed after it. Some weakness will probably remain in the knee; which will never be as strong as before the accident, but normal function will be almost complete. Strengthening the muscles after surgery is a key to full recovery; exercise is mandatory.

Injuries to the Anterior Cruciate Ligament

The anterior cruciate ligament prevents a forward shift of the knee joint. In most cases, it ruptures simultaneously with the medial collateral ligament in severe injuries to the knee, but occasionally, a sudden, violent twist will cause it to rupture alone (Illustration 18). This can happen when a slightly out-of-control player comes down hard on a foot and the spikes of his shoe get stuck in the ground causing the body to slide forward on the knee. It may feel as though something popped in the knee and the knee will then feel insecure. There may also be some swelling.

An isolated tear of this ligament is probably the hardest diagnosis to make because a knee examination at the time of injury can be perfectly normal. The knee may not rock or feel unstable to the examiner, and little or no swelling may be evident. But days, weeks, or months later swelling may occur and something will definitely seem to be wrong with the knee. Except for the swelling, it will look normal.

The most common incidental diagnosis made in knee surgery is probably that of an old tear of the anterior cruciate ligament. When

I operate on a knee for some other problem, I often see an old tear in this ligament.

Tears in the anterior cruciate ligament usually heal poorly, even if surgically repaired. But without surgery, they will never heal, under any circumstances. As we stated earlier, the anterior cruciate ligament prevents the forward shift of the leg under the knee. Once that ligament is torn, laxity and insecurity in the knee develop and tend to increase as time goes on. An athlete will gradually lose confidence in the knee and will be unable to make certain moves on it.

When both the anterior cruciate and medial collateral ligaments are ruptured, it is easy to see why the results of surgery on knee ligament injuries are not always very good. These two ligaments, and the medial meniscus, are so often injured together that they are called the "unholy" or the "unhappy" triad.

Orthopedic surgeons try to improve ways of getting the anterior cruciate ligament to heal. Many operations on old injuries, reconstructions, and rerouting operations are done to make up for old tears or the removal of this ligament. It is still accepted practice to remove the ligament once it is torn because the loose ends won't heal and sometimes get caught in the knee joint, causing it to lock. Some athletes with torn anterior cruciate ligaments are still able to function almost normally, but they are exceptions.

Injuries to the Posterior Cruciate Ligament

The posterior cruciate ligament prevents a backward shift of the knee and is much more rarely injured than the anterior cruciate ligament. Generally, a rupture only occurs from a severe injury to the knee (Illustration 18). While normal or even near normal function is rare once the ligament has been torn, it will usually heal quite well with surgical help.

Injuries to the Lateral Collateral Ligament

The lateral collateral ligament, on the outer side of the knee, is almost never ruptured. To do so would require a blow from the inside of the leg, something that rarely happens. But if it is injured, the ligament does not heal as well as the medial collateral ligament, and the results of surgery on it are not as good. Nevertheless, an early operation is clearly necessary to correct a rupture.

Posterior Capsule Injuries

Injuries that occur solely to the posterior capsule (the ligaments behind the knee) from forcing the leg up beyond a straight position (hyperextension) usually heal quite well, as long as no other ligament is ruptured. Ice and ten days to six weeks of rest should restore function to normal. If severe pain persists, casting may be necessary; it is a very effective way of relieving the pain. However, injuries associated with the ruptures of other ligaments frequently need surgical repair.

Injuries to the Front of the Knee

Loss of the ability to straighten out a knee or lift a leg indicates significant injury to the front of the knee, either a ruptured tendon or a fractured patella (kneecap). These are genuine emergencies and must be seen within twenty-four hours by a physician or an orthopedic surgeon. Surgery is usually required.

Direct blows to the kneecap are not always associated with swelling, and they can cause a great deal of pain. They mostly occur in collision sports, contact sports, falls, and auto accidents (as the so-called dashboard knee). Normally the undersurface of the kneecap is perfectly smooth, but this kind of injury can dent or crack it, leading to abnormal function, grating (a slight crunching), and pain. X-ray readings are usually normal in such cases. Although there may be no swelling, a bruise may appear over the front of the knee for a few days. The pain can be disabling for as long as six to twelve months before it disappears. If the knee has not improved completely by that time, it can be assumed that further medical or surgical treatment will be necessary.

Self-defense courses teach this type of blow to the patella because it is painful and very disabling. Provided there is no swelling and the knee can be straightened, medical attention is not usually necessary. Treatment consists of ice packs and aspirin until the pain and swelling subside. This treatment is applicable even if the pain is moderate or occasionally severe.

Other Knee Injuries

A procedure frequently mentioned in the newspapers is the flushing out of loose bone or cartilage chips from the knee joint. These occur as the result of trauma to a joint surface, frequently from a torn meniscus or a chip fracture of the kneecap. Bits of cartilage in the knee fluid reflect degeneration and the wearing of a joint surface and they are frequently a sign that early arthritis is beginning in the knee. If the area of abnormal joint surface is not extensive, surgical attempts to correct it by shaving off the rough area can at times be successful in younger people. But once the process starts it's almost always irreversible and leads to arthritis.

Postoperative Knee Trouble

If a problem develops after recovery from knee surgery, it is rarely an emergency, unless the pain is severe or another serious injury has been suffered. Most people do not realize that after knee surgery they are married to a lifetime of exercise to keep the knee strong. Failure to keep up the exercises outlined by the physician may result in swelling, giving way, pain, or instability in the knee. To determine if support for the knee is strong enough, stand in front of a full-length mirror with bare legs and tighten the quadriceps muscles, the large thigh muscles in the front. If one of them is especially weak, it will definitely look smaller than the other. There is little value in seeking an orthopedic consultation in this situation, since the first thing you will be told is that the knee is weak and you will need to do exercises to strengthen it. If you begin by doing exercises until the thighs become equal in size again, chances are the knee symptoms will be minimal and you will need no further consultation. But if trouble should persist even after exercise produces thighs of equal strength, then orthopedic consultation should be sought.

New surgical techniques may eventually result in quicker recovery after surgery. A major instrument of the future will be the arthroscope, a small fiberoptic telescope that enables a surgeon to look inside the knee and accurately diagnose a problem. Even some minor surgical procedures can be done through the arthroscope, thus eliminating large incisions and additional formal surgery. As more micro-instruments are perfected, many operations, including meniscus removal, will almost certainly be accomplished more efficiently.

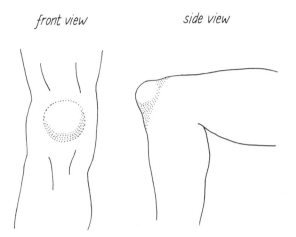

front view   *side view*

19/Prepatellar bursitis, or "housemaid's knee"

Swelling in Front of the Kneecap

Prepatellar bursitis, or swelling in front of the kneecap (housemaid's knee), is an athletic injury derived from falling on or scraping the kneecap. Swelling occurs in front of or on top of the kneecap (Illustration 19). It is a common problem and, though it looks awful, is usually not at all disabling.

Since this injury frequently occurs on artificial turf, players on that surface should be encouraged to wear knee pads that will cover the knees even when they are bent. Such prevention is far better than the cure. If such an injury is marked by deep abrasions and there is any possibility at all of infection, or if the swelling is extreme, medical consultation is necessary. For mild and moderate swelling with no pain and no loss of function, apply ice and wrap the injury with basketball player's knee pads or an elastic bandage. Given no further injury, the swelling should subside within ten days to two weeks, at which time normal activity can be resumed.

Note that the skin over the kneecap is extremely loose and a small amount of bleeding in this area will cause substantial swelling. In older athletes, repeated falls or swelling that stays prominent in this area may become a chronic disability.

Breaststroker's knee

The whip kick developed in the modern breaststroke calls for a turning out of the leg from the knee down. This turning of the leg with an explosive kick backward and outward causes repetitive stress along the inner side of the knee. A similar kick is also used occasionally by soccer players. It is obvious that the mechanics of the kick cause the problem for breaststrokers. But authorities on breaststroker's knee differ as to what actually happens in the knee and name at least ten possibilities. The four which follow are the most common:

1 / The medial collateral ligament becomes strained as the result of repetitive stress causing irritation and pain along the ligament (Illustration 18).

2 / Tendinitis develops in the three main tendons, (pes anserinus or duck's foot) that curve along the inner side of the knee and attach to the leg (Illustration 21). In a sense, this is hamstring tendinitis, which can occur in many sports, but is probably most common among breaststrokers. Pain experienced at the inside of the leg, below the knee joint, is a symptom of this tendinitis.

3 / Diffuse irritation develops, without swelling, throughout the entire knee joint from the repetitive bending and straining of the kick.

4 / The extreme rotation and bending of the leg causes the whole meniscus to dislocate out of the joint. This may lead to an acute locking of the knee, which may unlock after a few minutes or hours when the meniscus slips back into place. The knee will then be perfectly normal. (See page 85.) If this only happens once without any residual symptoms, swelling, or disability, and if total recovery follows, then medical care may not be necessary. However, if the condition becomes repetitive, and certainly if it is disabling, orthopedic consultation is mandatory and surgery may be required. I personally believe that if this situation occurs only once a season and is not disabling, it can be ignored.

The treatment for these possible problems in breaststroker's knee is ice, plus a decrease in the amount of breaststroke training. To avoid breaststroker's knee, two well-known authorities on the subject state categorically that swimmers should train for no more than ten months a year on that stroke.

Other Causes of Knee Pain

If constant pain is experienced in the knee, but there is no known injury or the knee locks up, or it feels as though something is moving around inside the knee, medical evaluation is necessary. These are all indications of problems. Pain experienced nightly should also be brought to the attention of a doctor, because it can signify a serious knee or hip condition. Frequently there is no explanation for occasional night pain, however.

One last word of caution: Knee pain without any evidence of knee disease is sometimes related to hip disorders.

12 / Thighs, Hips, and Pelvis

Thigh Injuries

ANY injury to the thigh that causes deformity or marked pain is best treated by comfortable splinting and transportation to an emergency room. This type of problem is best handled by paramedics, a trainer, or someone experienced in dealing with the victims of serious accidents. To avoid the risk of further aggravating the injury, it is best to keep the person comfortable while someone else calls for an ambulance. Above all, don't pull on any deformed part, since the risk of causing more damage is much greater than any possible benefit.

Bruises

Mild and not-disabling bruises and contusions to the thigh are most effectively treated with ice. A mild bruise by definition permits full and complete motion of the knee and hip. Deep massage is not good treatment and may aggravate the problem. Deeper bruises result in a limitation of movement at the knee or hip. For these, the best treatment is ice and rest until full motion is restored. This could take three days to three months. If there is any significant restriction of knee or hip motion, or marked swelling, and the athlete is unable to walk or lift the leg without help, then medical consultation must be sought within twenty-four hours.

Repeated blows to the front part of the thigh, which in football are often caused by loose thigh pads, may result in recurring bruises within the thigh muscle. This, in turn, sometimes leads to the development of a calcium deposit and then to a bony mass (myositis ossificans). If motion becomes restricted after repeated bruising, it is wise to seek medical consultation to see if such calcium deposits are forming. This type of injury must be treated with rest because exercise, when there is limited motion, will aggravate a deep bruise and may cause a bone mass to form. If that happens, it is definitely disabling and will require several months of rest.

Neglecting to impart a history of repeated bruising to a physician may lead him to confuse this condition with a malignant bone tumor. It is another instance where every bit of information you supply can be extremely helpful. A doctor should know in detail how the injury or pain developed and with what sport it is connected. Follow-up X-ray examinations of this type of injury may very well be necessary.

Muscle Pulls or Ruptures

Injuries to the front thigh muscles are common, especially in the region of the hip joint (Illustration 20). Like most muscle injuries, they

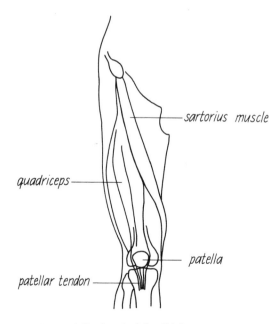

20/Important anatomy at the front of the thigh

take three to six weeks to heal. If the athlete is unable without help to lift a leg while keeping it straight, surgery may be needed, and medical consultation should be sought within twenty-four hours.

Hamstring Pulls or Ruptures

Almost everyone has heard of a pulled hamstring. Actually the hamstring is a large group of muscles at the back of the thigh (Illustration 21).

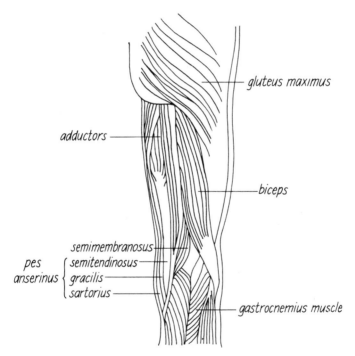

21/Hamstring and calf muscles. The adductor, biceps, semimembranosus, semitendinosus and gracilis make up the hamstring muscle group.

By definition, a hamstring pull is a tear in some part of the hamstring muscle group. Occasionally, the term also refers to a tear in one or more of the tendons connecting the hamstring muscles to the bones. The more severe the tear, the longer it will take to heal.

Hamstring pulls are very common in people who fail to warm up sufficiently and then sprint or run forcefully. Sprinters and hurdlers are especially vulnerable when training outdoors on winter days or on cool, brisk, breezy spring days. They are often underdressed and either fail to warm up properly or do not keep warm enough.

Hamstring pulls may also be the result of a serious misstep. When this happens, the quadriceps muscles may pull the hamstring muscles apart, if they are much stronger than the latter, or the hamstring muscles can pull themselves apart, if they contract violently.

The strength ratio of the quadriceps to the hamstring muscles is normally 60:40. If the quadriceps muscle in one thigh can lift seventy pounds but the hamstring can only lift thirty, a hamstring pull is very likely to occur. The best way to prevent such a pull is to avoid strengthening the quadriceps without also working on the hamstring muscles in any weight-lifting activities.

As always, the best treatment is prevention. Be sure to take the following essential steps before engaging in any strenuous activity:

1 / Warm up properly, especially on cool days early in the season. If necessary, prolong the wearing of a sweatsuit; don't try to impress anyone by simply wearing shorts on a cool day.

2 / Do adequate stretching exercises.

3 / After proper testing for any significant imbalance of muscle strength, do appropriate weight-lifting and strengthening exercises.

If a hamstring pull occurs and there is marked pain or you can see a bunching up of muscles, seek medical consultation. Rest, ice, and aspirin should be sufficient for mild pain. If there is any question, however, see a doctor within a reasonable period of time, twenty-four to seventy-two hours. Meanwhile, use ice and *rest.*

Rest is still the treatment of choice. For a mild pull, this means refraining from sprinting, and, possibly, from all running. Jogging may be attempted if it causes no discomfort, but hard sprinting must be eliminated for a week or two.

A moderate or severe hamstring pull will require a minimum recovery period of three weeks (six is more usual) before sporting activities can be resumed. At every Olympics one or two of our world-class sprinters are unable to participate because of hamstring pulls that need more time to heal. There is no way to speed up the natural healing process.

Other Thigh Pain

Pain down the front or side of the thigh, unaccompanied by an obvious injury (this includes knee pain with no apparent cause), may very well come from the hip joint. This should always be considered in people who complain of anterior (front) thigh pain. Pain in the back (posterior) part of the thigh, or tight hamstrings may be the result of a back problem. Anyone who complains of pain or tightness in both hamstrings would be wise to have a back examination. This is especially valid for a person with tight hamstrings who, while lying prostrate, cannot lift a leg ninety degrees, either alone or with help, regardless of whether or not there is a history of injury (Illustration 22). Refer to Chapter 13 for further discussion of back pain.

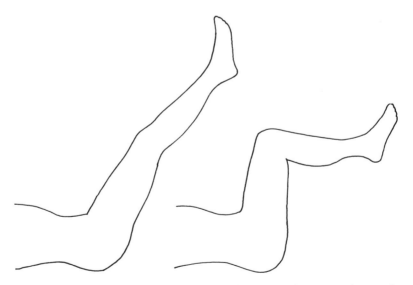

22/A test for a hamstring, hip, or back problem. If the legs cannot be raised perpendicular to the ground, when you are lying prostrate, you may have a back, hip, or hamstring problem. If the thighs can be raised at a 90° angle, with the knee bent, it is likely that the hip is fine.

Hip Injuries

An initial word of caution: Any significant injury of the hip in which the leg is deformed or the hip is fixed in one position for more than a few moments is best treated by going to an emergency room for a thorough evaluation. Any fracture or dislocation of the hip in a youngster or young adult is serious. These conditions are best treated immediately in a hospital.

Injury to the Front of the Hip

It is hard to watch a football game on television without hearing at least once that a player has a "hip pointer." This lay term relates to any severe, painful injury to the front part of the hip joint region (Illustration 23).

The anatomy of this area is complex. Two major nerves, one major artery, and at least one major vein all course under a very tight ligament in the vicinity of an exposed bony prominence. Several muscles that extend to the thigh also start there. Injury to any one of these structures, especially to the two nerves where they run under the ligament, can cause severe disabling pain which may last for anywhere from a moment to hours.

Emergency treatment with ice is all that is needed initially if there is no apparent deformity. If the pain gradually subsides in less than an hour and the athlete can either lift the leg at a ninety-degree angle while lying on the ground (Illustration 22) or hold it out straight while sitting on a chair, the hip pointer can be classified as mild.

If the pain subsides rapidly and a recovery of full motion is made with no loss of sensation, a return to athletic endeavor should be safe. Following loss of sensation, it is reasonable to seek medical consultation, although it is likely that this is a temporary condition. If the injured person is unable to lift the leg straight in the air while prostrate, a partial or complete rupture of one of the muscles that begin on the front of the hip joint may have occurred and medical treatment is needed.

Any deformity or loss of motion requires emergency treatment because of the potential seriousness of hip injuries. In fact, the disability may not be a hip pointer at all. To reiterate, any injury near the hip in which motion is extremely painful or limited and which lasts more

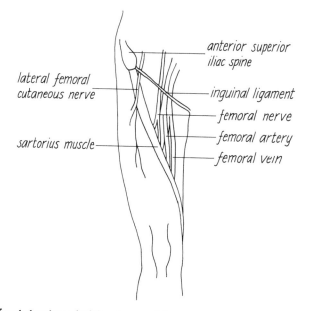

23/Hip-front structure. An injury to any of the structures concentrated in the upper area of the leg can be quite painful. The common football injury known as a hip pointer usually involves one or more of the following: the lateral femoral cutaneous nerve, sartorius muscle, anterior superior iliac spine (bony prominence at the front of the hip), and the femoral nerve. Injury to a nerve can cause severe pain or numbness in the thigh.

than a few minutes is best evaluated in an emergency room by a physician or an orthopedic surgeon.

Snapping, or "Dislocating," Hip

A snapping hip is not a common problem. Some people claim that their hip dislocates or pops in and out of joint. Women complain of it more than do men because they have a wider pelvis. An easy diagnosis can be made by placing your hand on the bony prominence at the widest part of the hip, and then having the person move the hip so it snaps or pops; frequently you can feel or even hear it. This noise is caused by a ligamentous structure, the fascia, as it slides over the bony prominence (greater trochanter) of the hip; the hip does not actually dislocate, or "pop in and out of joint." This benign condition is usually best ignored.

If a woman is truly disabled by this problem, it probably requires orthopedic consultation. Frustration from lack of improvement over a period of months or years may lead to surgery. Make sure to seek at least two opinions before going ahead with surgery, however, especially if a girl is anxious to have it, because an operation is of benefit only in rare instances.

Injuries to the Buttocks and Genitalia

Bruises to the buttocks are common but not usually severe. However, a direct blow to the male or female genitalia may be quite painful. If there is bruising or swelling, coupled with marked pain, or any tears or bleeding, medical evaluation should be obtained immediately. Ice is good first aid.

It is virtually impossible for a coach or parent to properly evaluate the injury of a female athlete who has been kicked in the genitalia since it is extremely difficult even for a physician in the emergency room to do so. Anesthesia may be required for a proper examination to be sure no significant tears are present. Therefore any significant painful injury with possible tearing or marked bruising should be evaluated by a gynecologist as soon as feasible. Ice, if tolerable, is a safe first aid treatment.

Blows to the male genitalia are usually prevented in collision and contact sports by the wearing of a protective cup. However, such injuries do occur. Frequently, the adolescent male hides this type of injury from his coach and parents. Marked bruising and swelling of the testicles may not be called to the parents' attention for a week or two. Unfortunately, that condition may result in the loss of the organ's function. These are serious injuries, and an emergency evaluation must be obtained immediately if there is marked bruising and bleeding into the scrotal sac. It is possible that emergency surgery will save the testicle.

Bruising of the penis is extremely rare, but if it shows marked swelling or bruising, emergency treatment should be sought. Normally, these conditions would be so painful that no male would hesitate to have an examination. But boys will sometimes say they have a groin pull when, in fact, they have a genital injury. If there is any question about it, ask a boy if he got kicked in the balls. This may sound crude, but you will probably get an honest answer by being so direct.

Athletic Supporters

One of the unasked and unanswered questions in athletics concerns the benefit of an athletic supporter. Boys in junior high and older are frequently warned that they must wear an athletic supporter or risk rupture, serious damage, or loss of male function. Actually the value of wearing a supporter for athletics is limited. A supporter should only be worn for comfort. In fact, many men have found a supporter to be uncomfortable for jogging and other running sports, especially if the straps cause chafing. The protective cup that players in collision sports wear is an entirely separate issue, and any time there is a significant risk of a collision, such a cup is valuable protection.

Numb Penis

A common problem in male cyclists who have traveled more than forty miles at a steady pace is loss of sensation in the penis and possibly the scrotum as well. This is due to pressure on the sensory nerves to both these areas. The condition is called ischemic neuropathy or anesthesia of the penis.

It is estimated that 50 percent of males who cycle forty miles or more will develop this problem. The numbness or loss of sensation completely disappears overnight, and full sensitivity and function are recovered without any permanent disability. There is no evidence that this numbness is harmful. Almost certainly it is a benign condition, similar to a numb leg that develops from sitting too long in one position.

Frostbite of the Penis

The term used by experienced joggers in the north and Midwest to describe very mild, first degree frostbite of the penis is "frozen popsicle." This condition is common among inexperienced joggers who go out in cold weather, especially on windy, below-freezing days, and then sweat through their jogging or running outfits and continue to run while soaking wet.

If a runner ignores the increasingly cold discomfort between his legs for long, he will develop this condition. As the minutes pass, it becomes increasingly uncomfortable, and usually forces him inside. Severe frostbite should not occur unless someone is out for hours after the onset of pain.

Recovery is usually rapid, a matter of a few minutes once rewarming occurs, but the recovery phase is extremely disagreeable. Runners have learned to avoid soaking through and to not overdress in cold weather. The one-piece orienteering suits that are worn in Scandinavia will probably become popular in the United States within a few years and will help to prevent this condition.

Frostbite at the tip of the penis has also been reported by bicyclists. Cyclists move at great speed with their legs separated, and are thus exposed to wind chill. Again, protection is the rule of the day.

Injuries to the Coccyx, or Tailbone

Injuries to the coccyx almost always result when an athlete lands in a sitting position on a hard surface, usually after having been knocked off his or her feet. The condition is much more common in a thin athlete than it is in a well-padded one. The pain is usually localized above the center of the buttocks (Illustration 24).

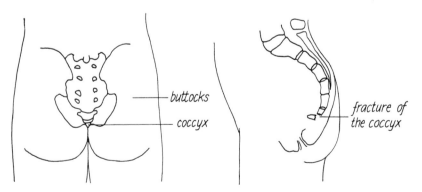

24/A fractured coccyx. Prolonged tenderness in the area of the coccyx (tailbone) may signify a fracture. Unless the coccyx is clearly fractured in two pieces, which is rare, the fracture is often hard to read on an X ray.

If the pain is only mild to moderate, applying ice for twenty-four to seventy-two hours should make it disappear. Once most of the pain is gone, soaking in a hot tub may be comforting, though it may cause some swelling and is not as effective as ice. Sitting on a pillow or cushion is also advisable. If the pain lasts longer than seventy-two hours, it is reasonable to seek medical care, although actually there is very little a doctor can offer—other than sympathy, pain relievers, ice, and the suggestion of sitting on a pillow. If the pain is marked, however, medical evaluation and probably X rays are warranted within twenty-four hours, although the treatment may still be the same as in the mild to moderate cases.

13 / Back and Neck

Sacrum Injuries

INJURIES between the tailbone and the lower portion of the back-bone most often occur from being kicked and can be extremely painful (Illustration 25). These injuries to the coccyx and sacrum may be tender for three weeks to three months, depending upon the sever-ity of the blow and age of the patient. If the pain is only mild and there is minimal bruising, treat with ice and rest. If the pain is moderate, or bruising is moderate to marked and there is swelling in the area, or there is any numbness in the buttocks or between the legs, medical evaluation, including X rays, is warranted. However, even if there is a fracture, treatment will probably be rest, ice, and pain relievers.

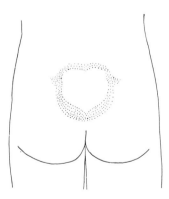

25/Fractured sacrum. Tenderness and bruising or swelling in the area above the coccyx, circled, may indicate a fractured sacrum. This injury is usually more severe than a fractured coccyx.

Lower Back Injuries

Back pain is not very common in the young and, when present, is usually a sign of a significant injury or problem.

In cases of severe low-back injury with pain that extends into the legs and an obvious disability the athlete should be transported by experienced paramedics or ambulance attendants to the nearest emergency room.

Bruises to the back are usually mild and not disabling and can be treated with ice. It is fairly safe to state that back pain lasting for more than twenty-four to seventy-two hours should be evaluated by a family practitioner or an orthopedic surgeon before resumption of any sports.

Direct injury to the back may cause a fracture of the spinous process on one of the lower vertebrae (Illustration 26). This condition will usually respond to three to six weeks of rest. It is painful but not serious. However, no one should ever guess about this diagnosis because it can only be proved with X rays. If pain lasts for more than twenty-four to seventy-two hours, see a doctor.

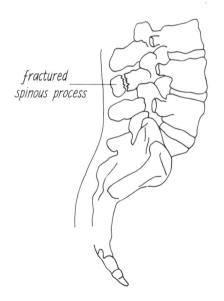

fractured spinous process

26/Fractured spinous process. A forced, sudden bending or a direct blow can fracture a spinous process, one of the relatively unimportant bony projections on a vertebra.

A second type of minor fracture is probably the most frequent spinal injury I see. It occurs in athletes who have had a forceful pull on a thigh muscle. The athlete might have come down hard while doing splits or have been in a position that forced the spine to bend backward. Either of these movements may result in a pull-off fracture of a transverse process (the bony projection at each side of a vertebra), but the diagnosis can only be made with an X ray (Illustration 27). In spite of the fact that the spine is fractured, all that is required for healing in most young athletes is three to six weeks of rest.

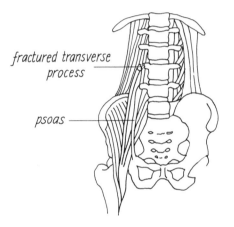

fractured transverse process

psoas

27/Pull-off fracture of a transverse process. A sharp or forced bend backward or the splits can cause a "pull-off" fracture. This type of fracture occurs when a bone is weaker than the tendons or ligaments to which it is attached; if both are strongly pulled, the bone gives first. The injury is minor, but severely painful. The muscle commonly involved in this pull-off fracture is the psoas. It runs from the spine to the thigh, through the pelvis, and around the hip joint.

There are two major medical reasons that back pain should not be ignored in young athletes: spondylolysis and spondylolisthesis. Spondylolysis is a medical term used to describe a fracture or failure of the main arch that supports and maintains the alignment of the spinal column and protects its nerves. Spondylolysis may be a stress fracture of the spine, occurring from repetitive forceful hyperextension or backbend activities. It is probably experienced by as many as 10 percent of all female gymnasts who do frequent backbends, and by football players, especially interior linemen, who perform various blocking maneuvers associated with a three-point stance. Trampolinists, pole vaulters, and swimmers who specialize in the butterfly stroke are also particularly vulnerable to this problem.

Spondylolysis first appears as a back pain, either from one acute injury or insidiously. If diagnosed early and accompanied by rest—at least three months away from the offending activity—there is good evidence that most of the condition will heal, resulting in a normal back. The problem occurs when an athlete continues to play while experiencing pain. If he or she ignores it, either through dedication to the sport or because an eager coach or parent pushes too hard, the defect will not heal. Instead, it will be the cause of continuing back pain during vigorous activities, and, worse, it may very well lead to the second condition mentioned, spondylolisthesis.

In spondylolisthesis, the entire spinal column slips forward, usually because both sides of its main supporting arch have become too weak to hold it (Illustration 28). During vigorous activity, spondylolisthesis may cause disabling low-back pain. On the other hand, it may be painless and cause a simple tightening of the hamstrings due to the forward slippage of the vertebrae, one upon the other. Some team physicians have indicated that approximately one-third of all NFL interior linemen have this back condition. While there are times that these athletes experience only a mild aching back, it is quite apparent that mechanically the back is no longer normal. As a general rule, the

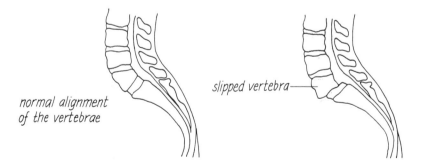

normal alignment of the vertebrae

slipped vertebra

28/Spondylolisthesis: Repeated hyperextension (bending back) of the spine, in spite of back pain, is likely to cause spondylolisthesis. This is a true mechanical weakening of the spine in which the arch supporting the lowest lumbar vertebra weakens to the extent that the whole spinal column slips permanently forward. Those most vulnerable to this condition are female gymnasts, football linemen, trampolinists, pole vaulters, and swimmers who specialize in the butterfly stroke.

condition precludes any vigorous lifting or heavy work, which will cause backache. If the spondylolisthesis is progressive and disabling, corrective surgery may very well be necessary.

My detailed discussion of the above was not intended to make you a diagnostician of spondylolysis and spondylolisthesis, but to point out the fact that back pain can indicate or lead to a severe problem and should never be ignored, especially in the presence of tight hamstrings. (See Illustration 21.)

Lower Back Pain and Slipped Discs

Back pain is the most common cause of disability and loss of time from work in the United States. By all accounts, it has reached epidemic proportions, although for the most part, the pain does not begin until after a person reaches the mid-twenties. While there are many good books on the subject, there is still a great deal of misunderstanding about back pain, or backache.

Back pain is commonly a disease of affluence. It is virtually unknown in developing countries except among the upper classes. The main differences between our affluent society and people who are less well off in other parts of the world are the automobile and obesity. Peasants walk everywhere they go and as a group are generally underweight. We tend to ride everywhere we go and, as a nation, we are overweight. The automobile is detrimental in two ways: it deprives us of valuable walking exercise, and some scientific evidence indicates that repetitive bouncing in a car over a long period of time is probably harmful.

Lifting brings on most episodes of back pain. Whether it is a tennis ball or a 250-pound set of barbells, lifting with one's back can cause an acute attack of back pain. Adding a twisting motion puts even more stress across the back. Therefore, any lifting should be done with bent knees, and no twisting motion.

Most often the pain in backache comes from an intervertebral disc: such discs act as shock absorbers between the vertebrae of the spine. Occasionally an unusual strain or the combination of weak muscles and a strain makes a disc bulge so much that it presses, or pinches, one of the nerves to the leg, creating severe pain in that area as well. Many ligaments, small muscles, and joints in the lower back are also prone to injury or strain that can cause back pain radiating down the leg, even if no pressure is actually exerted on a nerve to the leg. Pain that runs from the back into the leg independent of a pinched nerve is called somatic referred pain.

Among the terms used to describe backache and back pain are muscle strain, muscle pull, pulled back, wrenched back, degenerating disc, slipped disc, deteriorating disc, bulging disc, herniated disc, and sciatica. Most of these are different lay or medical terms for describing back pain that may or may not radiate down the back of the legs. True sciatica is back pain associated with pain that radiates down through the back of the buttocks all the way to the foot.

Over 90 percent of all people with lower back pain will recover with adequate rest and time. The rest may vary from simply eliminating the offending activity to complete bed rest at home or in a hospital. Full recovery may take anywhere from a few to many months, depending on the severity of the problem.

The following types of back pain demand medical evaluation:

1 / Severe, disabling pain that is impossible to relieve with rest and aspirin or an acetaminophen, such as Tylenol or Datril.

2 / Lower back pain associated with fever. This combination often signifies some other type of medical problem and should never be ignored.

3 / Lower back pain associated with difficulty in urinating or, worse, the inability to urinate, which may involve severe pressure on the nerves to the bladder. The condition demands prompt medical attention. *Caution:* Since straining of any kind will frequently increase the pain of most common backaches, people are sometimes fearful of urinating or moving their bowels, though they may not have lost the ability to do so.

4 / Back pain coupled with weakness in the foot or a leg.

5 / Back pain that is worse at night in bed, or at rest. This is not typical of the common backache, and is probably not an emergency situation, but it should be examined.

After recovering from an attack of back pain, a sensible, nonaggravating exercise program must be undertaken to prevent recurrence and to decrease the severity of any future attack. If back pain is uncommon in athletes and peasants, it is logical to assume that better fitness decreases the chances of its occurring. The YMCA has developed a fine exercise program for people recovering from episodes of back pain, and I strongly recommend that program, with a warning that holds true for any exercises: *Do not attempt an exercise that is painful.*

Sit-ups with the knees bent are particularly good for tightening and strengthening the abdominal muscles, which are so important in keeping the back strong. In most adults, these muscles are weak and in poor tone.

The single best activity for strengthening the muscles that support the back is swimming. But avoid the butterfly stroke, which can be painful. Swimming strengthens all the correct muscles while the buoyancy of the water relieves some of the normal stresses of gravity on the body. Walking and jogging, if comfortable, are also good for strengthening the proper muscles. Cycling, though less helpful, will strengthen some of the large muscles in the back of the thighs.

Tennis and golf are two of the most difficult sports to resume after an attack of back pain because they require a great amount of twisting that puts a significant stress across the back. These sports should not be taken up again until recovery is complete.

Scoliosis, or Curvature of the Spine

Scoliosis is actually a developmental problem that occurs most frequently in early-teenage girls. If there is any question of your child's having curvature of the spine, medical evaluation (including X rays) by a physician or orthopedic surgeon should be obtained.

The easiest way to check for scoliosis is to have the child bend over at the waist with a bare back, while you carefully judge the straightness of the spine from directly behind her or him. Surprisingly, a severe curve can develop without a family's noticing, since teenagers' backs are bared primarily in a bathing suit during the summer months.

Certainly if there is scoliosis in a family history, a parent should check a child's spine every six to twelve months for this problem. Again, if there is any question at all, medical attention is warranted, but not on an emergency basis.

Upper Back Pain

Upper back pain, unless it is in the middle of the back right along the spine, is predominantly muscular. This type of pain is frequently associated with sports like swimming, baseball, tennis, and football, that require a lot of arm use. A mild, nondisabling pain in this region often occurs in swimmers who do not warm up properly, or who are fatigued or recovering from an illness. (See page 141 for a discussion on shoulder pain in swimmers.) A tennis player will often feel acute pain after failing to warm up and then trying to serve hard. The best treatment is ice and rest until the pain subsides. Anything more than mild to moderate pain is best evaluated by a physician.

Neck Injuries

Neck injuries are more feared than any other sports injury because, when severe, they are sometimes accompanied by partial or complete paralysis of the arms and legs. That is an extreme end of the spectrum, however. Most neck problems do not have devastating complications.

Anyone with an injured neck who complains of severe neck pain, especially if it is accompanied by pain, numbness, tingling, or a momentary burning sensation in the arms and/or legs, should be moved only by a doctor, trained paramedic, or the ski patrol if it's a skiing accident. If the mishap takes place anywhere near civilization, the injured person should be kept comfortable on the ground until properly trained help arrives. It is far better to let a person lie in the snow, mud, or rain for half an hour than to move him or her prematurely. Movement of the injured by someone who is inexperienced is highly risky; it increases the chance for paralysis and may condemn the person to total paralysis or even death.

On the football field, only a physician or someone specifically training about what to do should remove the helmet from a player with a neck injury—unless the athlete is experiencing extreme difficulty in breathing. It is best for paramedics to transport the player, helmet and all, to an experienced physician, an orthopedic surgeon, or a neurosurgeon, who can then cut off the helmet. Any attempt to remove one of the new tight-fitting helmets could be extremely damaging. Never try to remove a tight-fitting football helmet from someone who complains of neck pain following an injury.

A person injured on a trampoline should not be moved until experienced help arrives, even if he or she is dangling partway off it. Simply support the individual gently in that position until trained personnel arrive. The exception to not moving a person is, of course, a swimming accident where drowning is a possibility. In this case, it is best to hold the person suspended in the water, face-up, with the head tilted slightly back, until proper help can get there.

With luck you will never be around anyone who has just experienced a severe neck injury. But if you are, and the person is complaining of severe pain or stiffness in the neck, it should be seen by a doctor. If the person is literally holding his head and afraid to move it, take him immediately to the nearest emergency room for evaluation and treatment. Helpful support can be provided to the neck by wrapping it with one or two large towels to form a type of soft, bulky collar. Follow the same procedures as for someone who has neck pain accompanied by a burning sensation in the arms (see below). In both cases, keep the head as still as possible.

If a child mentions a neck injury, but has no present pain or restriction in moving the head and neck, no medical evaluation is necessary. Be sure to ask, however, if there had been any burning sensation in the shoulders, upper back, or arms, or any numbness and tingling in the arms and legs following the accident. If the answer is positive, follow the instructions in the next section.

Burning Sensation in the Arms

"Burners" is the lay term for an injury that causes electricitylike shooting sensations or pain from the neck into the arm, shoulder, or upper-back region. This symptom results from an injury, such as a blow from a hockey stick or a fall, that stretches the brachial plexus, a large group of nerves located between the neck and arm (Illustration 29). Usually the symptoms are only momentary. They are severe and quite frightening, but if there is no residual weakness and no neck injury, then only some mild muscle soreness will persist for a matter of hours and total recovery can be expected.

In more severe injuries to these nerves there will be some weakness in the muscles that move the shoulder or elbow. It may be quite harmful to return to play if there is any weakness in the shoulder or arm. The weakness may last for hours, days, or even many months; only rarely is it permanent. Healing simply takes time. Unfortunately, little else will speed up the healing process of a severe nerve injury.

If the athlete has no neck pain at all after an injury and can move the neck freely, then have him or her remove any shirt and raise the arms over the head. If the arms can be raised freely over the head, then have the athlete lean against a wall while you look at the shoulder

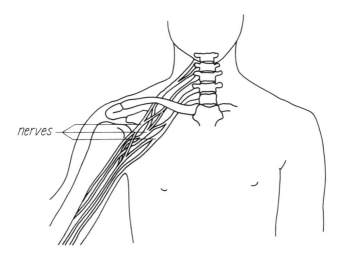

29/Brachial plexus. The major group of nerves running from the spine to the shoulder and arm is called the brachial plexus. Note how the nerves curve under the collarbone before continuing down the inner side of the arm.

blades (see Illustration 30). If one shoulder blade sticks out more than the other it indicates injury on that side to the long thoracic nerve. As long as there is free movement of the neck in all directions and no weakness or pain in the arms, medical consultation can be sought on an elective basis within the next day or two. However, if there is severe pain and limited motion, see a doctor right away. No player responding negatively to the above tests should resume playing without being medically evaluated.

Another cause of a burner is a ruptured disc in the neck (Illustration 31). Usually the athlete will have some degree of stiffness and pain in the neck and persistent pain in the shoulder and arm. This, of course, is serious and may require rest or intensive medical treatment if the pain does not subside within a matter of minutes. These symptoms call for a moratorium on sports until a medical examination is obtained. Diagnosis of this type of injury should only be made by a physician and is beyond the scope of this book.

I believe that frequently this type of neck injury is not reported to the coach or parent out of fear that play will no longer be permitted. Judging from football, where we have documentation, cervical disc injuries must be the most underreported injury of all. Thorough ques-

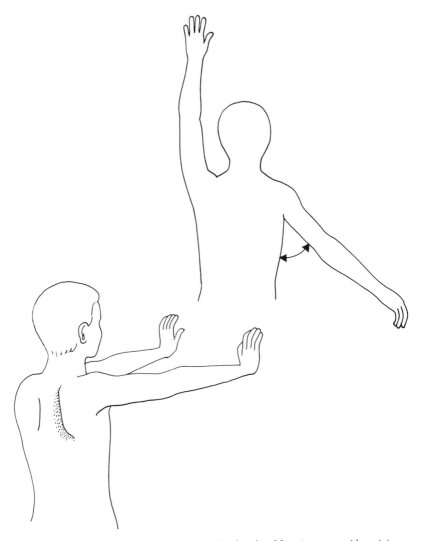

30/Evaluating nerve and tendon injuries in the shoulder. A person with an injury to a nerve or tendon in the shoulder is unable to lift the arm overhead. To determine injury of the long thoracic nerve to the shoulder muscles, have the injured person remove the shirt and push against a wall. The shoulder blade on the injured side may "wing" or stick out more than the other one, indicating injury. Even subtle problems show up with this test.

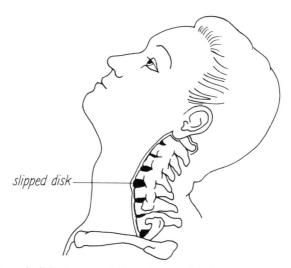

slipped disk

31/"Slipped" neck disk. A ruptured (slipped) cervical disk in the neck can cause severe neck and/or shoulder pain as well as arm pain or weakness, or, occasionally, just a stiff neck.

tioning of college football players and a reading of their X-ray examinations reveals that at least 10 percent of the freshmen who played high school football either have or had some kind of neck injury. Questioning these boys indicates that they routinely hid the neck injury from their coaches and parents. The "horse" or cervical collars worn by football players who have recovered from a neck injury often help prevent recurrences of neck trouble.

14 / Head and Face

Head Injuries

HEAD injuries are perhaps the most commonly ignored serious injuries in athletics. Often they are not taken seriously and, unfortunately, fatalities occur that could easily have been prevented.

"Dazed," "bell-rung," "out-on-his-feet," "knock-out" are all different ways of describing a concussion. By definition, a concussion is a head injury associated with a loss of consciousness or of the ability to recall ongoing or past events.

A person unable to remember events before the occurrence of an injury has what is called retrograde amnesia. An example would be the victim of an automobile accident who can't remember leaving home in the morning. If the same person also has difficulty remembering events that happened after the injury, their condition is called post-traumatic, or anterograde, amnesia. After receiving a severe blow some football players can't remember playing the rest of a game. The length of post-traumatic amnesia is one way of measuring the severity of the concussion.

Obviously, a concussion is not limited to a collapse into a coma. It is also clear that anyone who can describe exactly what happened at the moment of impact and afterward does not have a concussion. If the person does not remember an injury, or, worse than that, cannot remember what happened several seconds or longer before and after it occurred, he or she has suffered a concussion. Whether knocked unconscious or not, it was a concussion.

What happens in a concussion? Whenever the head receives a blow it swings back on the neck, and the brain, which can be compared to thick gelatin within the bony vault, shakes back and forth inside it. The more severely the brain bounces, the greater the injury. Extensive blows will cause hemorrhaging and death of brain cells, depending upon what part of the brain bounces against the skull. Sometimes slow bleeding into the cavity between the skull and the brain can cause increasing pressure on the brain, leading to potential coma and death.

Hourly observation is the most important treatment for any person who has had a concussion. That means every hour, night and day, for twenty-four hours, the victim must be talked to for several minutes to see that his or her speech and thought are intelligent and no loss of memory has occurred. During the night sleep should be interrupted on the hour. This precaution can mean the difference between life and death, because any pressure caused by the slow bleeding of a concussion can be relieved by a fairly simple neurological operation, if it is caught in time.

Certainly anyone who has been knocked totally unconscious must be transported to a hospital, but it takes an astute observer to pick up the subtle signs of a mild concussion. To prove a mild concussion in someone who has been hit hard (this happens predominantly in collision sports) ask if he remembers the hit. If that is impossible or the athlete seems dazed and confused, he has had a concussion. Unless this condition clears and the athlete becomes fully oriented as to where he is, knows what time it is, who the opponent is, and all the plays or moves he would normally know, he should not be permitted to return to a game under any circumstance. After suffering a concussion, a player should not be permitted to resume any activity, even if recovery seems complete, until cleared by a physician.

The following conditions demand immediate medical evaluation:

1/ An increasing headache after an injury.

2/ Blurred vision, difficulty seeing, or blindness.

3/ Staggering or difficulty with balance.

4/ Nauseousness or continuous vomiting.

5/ Sleep from which the person cannot be aroused.

Paying attention to these signs can save a life!

A person knocked unconscious who is not having difficulty breathing should be left lying on the ground until competent help can transport him to an emergency room. Since it's quite common for neck injuries to be associated with concussions and loss of consciousness, it is extremely important not to touch the neck. It is very dangerous to lift someone with a head injury and take him in the back seat of a car to an emergency room. Always wait for the experts to do this.

If the victim is having difficulty breathing, it is very important that an adequate airway be established. It would be extremely unusual for a trained athlete to have a heart attack, so cardiopulmonary resuscitation is not indicated if a pulse can be felt. In that case, the safest way to restore an airway is to pull up and backward on the jaw. Usually, an athlete will then breathe alone, without the need for mouth-to-mouth resuscitation.

Medical opinion differs as to how many concussions preclude further play in collision, or contact, sports. With full recovery and evaluation, most physicians will permit a player to return to a collision sport after a mild concussion. The difference of opinion arises with a second or third concussion. Some doctors feel strongly that resumption of collision sports after two concussions should not be permitted. After each concussion, the risk of serious injury and permanent brain damage becomes greater. The number of concussions a person can tolerate is a matter that should be decided by the individual and a neurosurgeon.

The risks involved with repeated concussions are the same as those taken by a boxer. The punch-drunk fighter, though parodied in some movies, is a tragic example of someone who has had multiple small concussions resulting in moderately severe brain damage. The damage can be permanent and clearly disabling.

Lest anyone think I am overdramatizing head injuries, every neurosurgeon in the country must have at least one story of a patient who, after a head injury, walked, talked, and seemed fine to most people, but later died rather suddenly of some intracranial complication stemming from the injury. Head injuries and concussions should not be taken lightly or ignored; the stakes are too high.

Astute football coaches have at times noticed players who begin to play poorly after receiving a severe blow. It is not uncommon for players on a team to realize that something is wrong with one of their members and then cover up the fact that the person seems dazed and is not fully aware of what is going on. I hope that education of players will prevent this, but I know many instances of football players who have played as much as three quarters of a game without being able to remember anything beyond the first quarter. These players have had concussions and should have been seen by a physician.

Eye Injuries

Most injuries to the eye are obvious, as is the need for treatment.

A person will know immediately if there is a small bit of dirt or other foreign body in the eye. With a steady hand, it is usually safe to gently remove the speck with a piece of cotton. It is even safer to flush the eye out with any of the sterile eye washes available. Another safe procedure is to look up under a gentle shower or stream of running water. If something is stuck in the eye, however, it should only be removed by an ophthalmologist.

The other common eye condition is a corneal abrasion, usually caused by a ball striking the surface of the eye. This is often quite painful and demands an immediate visit to an emergency room. Such injury can be completely prevented by wearing glasses or goggles. Since the advent of complete face guards in hockey, severe eye injuries have been eliminated; eyes are no longer being lost from a hockey puck or stick.

At present the two sports most frequently responsible for eye injuries are racquetball and tennis. A racquetball is almost the perfect size for seriously damaging the eye because it can fit right into the eyeball socket. All racquetball players should wear protective goggles or glasses.

Eye problems in tennis are usually the result of a mishit volley, when the ball comes off the player's own racket into his eye. It is the kind of accident that happens too quickly for any preventive reaction. The fuzz on the ball causes a corneal abrasion that will usually heal, but the injury is extremely painful and can be prevented by wearing goggles or glasses.

Corneal abrasions require medical treatment: serious cases should be taken to an ophthalmologist, minor ones can be handled by a physician. Any injury to the eye that causes partial or total loss of vision requires the immediate attention of an ophthalmologist. Any head injury with attendant loss of vision should be treated at once in an emergency room.

Nosebleeds

Most nosebleeds in athletes occur in the anterior (forward) part of the nose, and nine out of ten cases can satisfactorily be treated at the scene of the accident. If an athlete is struck in the nose and develops a nosebleed, take the following steps:

1 / Have the person sit up.

2 / Look carefully at the shape and position of the nose. If it is crooked or aligned differently than before the accident, it is probably broken and will need to be set. In this case apply a towel and ice pack and arrange surgical consultation. The best time to straighten a broken nose is in the first few hours or after three to four days. Swelling develops in a few hours and takes a few days to go away, during which time it is virtually impossible to set the nose.

3 / If the nose is straight, squeeze the front part tightly for fifteen minutes nonstop. This should control most bleeding. Squeezing with a small ice or cold pack is even better. If the bleeding lasts more than fifteen minutes, call a doctor or go to an emergency room. In the meantime, keep squeezing the nose to control the bleeding somewhat.

4 / If you are a long way from medical care, a cotton ball coated with petroleum jelly can be placed in the very front part of each nostril. Then squeezing the front part of the nose for ten to fifteen minutes may stop the bleeding.

Ear Injuries

Any injury to the ear in which there is loss of hearing or dizziness demands immediate consultation with an ear, nose, and throat specialist or a speedy visit to an emergency room. The same is true of injuries to the external ear (the anatomical term for that part of the ear we can see) that cause swelling or bruising. They can lead to a permanently misshapen, or cauliflower, ear if not treated as an emergency. Ice applied at the scene of the accident will help control some of the swelling.

Swimmer's Ear

Swimmer's ear is a very common superficial skin infection that occurs in many swimmers regardless of age. It comes from spending long sessions in the water during which the protective skin oil and outer skin layers are actually washed away. This infection, known as pseudomonas otitis externa, can be extremely painful and disabling and tends to recur.

Any swimmer who complains of an earache in the outer ear probably has swimmer's ear. If so, a gentle tug on the ear will usually be very painful, and a green-colored discharge may ooze from the skin. In the event of other complications, such as fever, swelling, severe pain, or large amounts of drainage, see a physician. Otherwise, treat mild cases as follows:

Gently wash the ear three or four times daily with a mild (1 to 2 percent) boric acid solution or a 2 percent acetic acid solution. Household vinegar, which is usually 5 percent acetic acid, will also do. It can either be diluted with equal parts of water or, if not too painful, used full strength. If none of these treatments work within one to three days, see your physician.

Over-the-counter prescriptions for swimmer's ear are available, but read the labels. Some are only diluted rubbing alcohol, which is totally ineffective.

Throat Injuries

Direct injury to the larynx (voice box) is extremely painful and disabling. A frequent cause is clothes-lining (a blow across the front of the neck) in football, which should be condemned. Fortunately, such an injury is usually short-lived, and the pain resolves very quickly. If wheezing and difficulty in breathing persist, however, *immediate* emergency-room attention is vital. Even trained paramedics may not be able to help a serious injury to the larynx or voice box, so getting to the nearest emergency room may be a matter of life or death. Don't wait for anyone, just get to the hospital!

Injuries to the Face

Any injury to the face resulting in double vision or blurred vision needs attention by a physician, as does any painful injury to the jaw after which the person is unable to bite down. Put your fingers in the mouth and gently pull on the upper teeth. If that is not painful, pull on the lower teeth. If that is not painful, it's probably safe to assume no major injury has occurred to the jaw. Obviously, broken teeth should be seen by a dentist.

15 / Chest and Shoulders

Injuries to the Chest

SERIOUS injuries to the chest are extremely rare in athletics, but contusion, or bruising, of the chest wall is common. The chest wall consists of the sternum, or breastbone, the ribs, and the costal cartilage, which connects the ribs to the sternum (Illustration 32).

Anyone who complains of localized tenderness after an injury, with persistent pain when taking a deep breath, can probably be assumed to have a broken rib, until proved otherwise. It is unwise to permit someone who has pain on breathing to return to any type of sporting activity prior to evaluation by a physician. If the person experiences no difficulty in breathing, no shortness of breath, and the pain is only mild to moderate, contact a physician any time within 24 to 72 hours. Any shortness of breath or difficulty in breathing indicates the need for immediate medical attention.

Most rib fractures are mild and will heal without difficulty, but no athlete with a rib fracture should return to a sport without clearance from a physician. If the athlete has no trouble breathing, but the pain persists for more than 24 hours, in spite of icing it down, medical treatment may be necessary. However, this pain can become chronic and extremely disabling even after prolonged medical treatment.

"Having the wind knocked out" is the most common chest or abdominal injury in sports. This is usually a muscle spasm that makes breathing quite difficult for a very short period of time, but the athlete will recover after a while, get up, and be fine. If he or she has no difficulty in breathing, no pain on deep breathing, and is able to jog, run, and sprint comfortably, there is no reason to stop an activity.

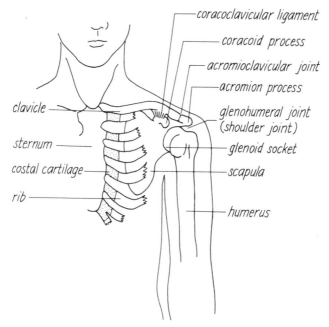

32/Front view of shoulder anatomy

Breast Injuries

Contusions of preadolescent and male breasts are no different from contusions anywhere else on the body. More developed breasts that sustain a contusion should be treated with ice and breast binders. Any injury to the breast that fails to respond to ice, binding, or support with a brassiere should be checked by a physician.

Abdominal Injuries

Consider any blow to the abdomen as an internal abdominal injury, unless proved otherwise. Obviously blows of minor force followed by no pain or disability can be ignored. However, any injury to the abdomen resulting in pain or disability must be seen by a physician. Internal injuries can be quite severe, and it is beyond the scope of this book to instruct anyone in how to evaluate and treat them.

Any severe injury or contusion to the back with resulting blood in the urine must be evaluated immediately by a physician, urologist, or emergency-room physician. In fact, any time blood is seen in the urine, this advice should be followed. Adolescents who have bloody urine often hide the fact from their parents, so if a youngster seems to be walking around rather stiffly, it is wise to find out exactly why. Anyone with difficulty urinating should also be seen immediately by a physician.

As a rule, it is only safe to let minor abdominal injuries go without medical consultation. Any time a serious and painful condition arises in the abdomen, it is safest to see a physician right away. If that is not possible, go to an emergency room.

Shoulder Girdle and Collarbone Injuries

The collarbone is formed by the two inner halves of the clavicles. On each side it joins with the sternum (breastbone) to form a sterno-

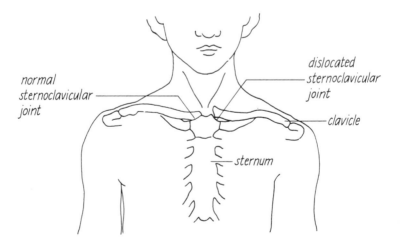

33/Dislocated sternoclavicular joint. A fall on the point of the shoulder sometimes results in a dislocated sternoclavicular joint.

clavicular joint, which is capable of rotating slightly (Illustration 33). This joint is frequently injured in hard falls when the body lands on the point of the shoulder and the force of the fall is transmitted through the clavicle to the sternum. Injuries to this joint are extremely painful and can be disabling for weeks. Anyone who has fallen directly on the end of a shoulder may experience agonizing pain in the chest area.

The injured person should be examined while still on the ground and with the shirt removed. If there is no marked swelling or depression in the collarbone area and both sides of the collarbone seem the same except for tenderness at the sternoclavicular joint, it is safe to simply apply ice packs for twelve to twenty-four hours before seeking medical consultation. If there is minor swelling and it disappears quickly, it is reasonable to continue icing the area two or three times a day for two to three days. Sporting activity can be resumed at that time, if tolerable, but the injury may require ten to twenty-one days of rest. This condition does not require medical attention. But the presence of an obvious deformity or marked swelling necessitates a medical consultation within twenty-four hours.

Any depression occurring in the area of the collarbone could indicate an extremely rare complication, a posterior (inward) dislocation. In other words, the collarbone could be dislocated into the chest. This is an extreme emergency condition that calls for immediate attention in an emergency room. Injuries to the sternoclavicular joint are difficult to treat, and any deformity may be permanent, regardless of treatment.

Injuries to the Main Part of the Clavicle

In most cases, injuries to the main part of the clavicle are fractures, and some authorities claim this to be the most common fracture of the childhood years. Until proved otherwise, the presence of swelling, tenderness, and possibly bruising indicate a fracture of the clavicle. Depending on the situation and comfort of the individual, ice packs and a sling may suffice as treatment until the following morning, when X rays should be taken. The diagnosis of a fractured clavicle is extremely easy to make under most circumstances. Severe pain or swelling in the arm requires immediate emergency consultation, however. Depending on the age of the athlete, a fractured clavicle may take from three weeks to two months to heal. There is no safe way for an injured person to return to sports until the bone has healed.

Shoulder Separations

A "shoulder separation" is an injury to the acromioclavicular joint (Illustration 34). The acromion (see Illustration 32) is a bony forward projection of the scapula (shoulder blade) that meets the outer end of the clavicle to form the acromioclavicular, or AC, joint. A second bony projection of the scapula, the coracoid process, rides beneath the clavicle and is connected to it by two very strong ligaments. Injuries to the AC joint generally affect these ligaments as well.

Shoulder separations are divided into three grades of severity. A Grade 1 injury, or partial shoulder separation, is limited to the AC joint alone. There is no deformity or displacement of the bones and no significant damage to the ligaments between the coracoid process and the clavicle. Examination reveals some tenderness over the AC joint and minor swelling. Grade 1 injuries are best treated with ice and, if

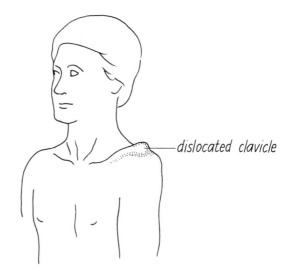
—dislocated clavicle

34/Typical Grade 3 shoulder separation. A hard fall on the point of the shoulder may result in a shoulder separation, known medically as an acromioclavicular dislocation. These separations are divided into three grades by degree of severity. The least severe condition, Grade 1, shows no deformity, little if any swelling, and some tenderness. Grade 2 (partial) and Grade 3 (complete) separations result in deformity, swelling, and pain.

necessary for comfort, a sling. This type of injury will usually be disabling for a period of 10 to 21 days; by then resumption of full sports activity is usually possible.

Grade 2 and Grade 3 injuries require medical consultation and treatment. In a Grade 2 injury the AC joint partially separates. There is also stretching and partial tearing of the ligaments between the coracoid process and the clavicle, causing marked pain, definite swelling, and perhaps some deformity. However, the injury can safely be treated for at least twenty-four hours with ice, rest, and a sling before seeing a physician, unless there is marked pain, numbness, or tingling in the hand and arms.

The reason it is so important to medically check a Grade 2 injury is that it can often be more disabling on a chronic basis than the more severe Grade 3 type. Because it may not look very bad and the bones may be only slightly out of place, the Grade 2 injury is sometimes not treated vigorously enough, or worse yet, it may not be recognized for what it is. If this happens, a permanent, painful condition of the AC joint will result.

To prevent a chronic problem, Grade 2 shoulder separations require eight weeks away from sports plus vigorous treatment with taping, splinting, or strapping, depending on the physician. Poor healing from this injury frequently causes chronic pain in the AC joint that leads to surgery. Unfortunately, this can happen even with the best care.

Grade 3 injuries to the AC joint are usually quite painful and obviously deforming. However, at times, it may be difficult to make a visual distinction between a Grade 2 and a Grade 3 injury, without the benefit of a specialized X-ray examination. In a Grade 3 injury the ligaments holding the clavicle in place are completely torn, as is the joint. This is a true dislocation of the AC joint or a complete shoulder separation. A few orthopedic surgeons advocate no treatment at all for this condition, since the injury will frequently become painless after two to three months. However, most recommend surgery to set the clavicle back in place correctly, repair the ligaments, and fix the joint. Under the careful scrutiny of a physician it is sometimes possible with vigorous taping and strapping to treat Grade 3 injuries without surgery. But the treatment must be intensive and adhered to for a period of at least two months. If the pain is tolerable after a Grade 3 injury occurs, medical attention can wait twenty-four hours, but a sling and ice should be used immediately.

Dislocation of the Shoulder Joint

The average person almost certainly confuses a shoulder separation and a shoulder dislocation. First, there are two joints at the shoulder, the AC or acromioclavicular joint, and the shoulder, or glenohumeral joint (Illustration 32). A shoulder separation involves the AC joint, and may actually refer to a dislocation. A shoulder dislocation is exactly that and refers only to the main shoulder joint. The main shoulder joint is formed by the humerus (the long bone of the upper arm) and the glenoid socket, the saucer-shaped pocket on the outer edge of the shoulder blade.

Like the knee joint, the shoulder joint is inherently unstable and requires strong ligaments to keep it from dislocating. A forceable backward bending of the arm will tend to twist the humerus out of the glenoid socket causing a typical anterior (forward) shoulder dislocation. When this happens, an athlete will feel and claim that the shoulder is out of joint and will complain of rather severe disabling pain in that area.

The first time this injury occurs to someone, it is best to have X rays and see a physician trained in treating these lesions. There are four reasons for this:

1/ It is virtually impossible to tell a shoulder dislocation from a high fracture with a totally displaced humerus. This type of fracture is common in growing adolescents and calls for different treatment.

2/ Injury to the nerves is quite possible and, if someone pulls on the shoulder, any resultant nerve damage might unjustly be blamed on the pull rather than on the accident itself.

3/ X rays will also show if there are any minor fractures associated with the dislocated shoulder and reveal on which side the humerus came out of the shoulder joint, front or back.

4/ Anyone but a trained physician might fail to put the bone back in the joint, inflicting pain with no resulting benefit. In fact, once an attempt has failed, the second try by a medical expert is often more difficult because the injured person is more anxious and in more pain. Only if you are far from treatment and you are sure it is a forward dislocation and that some attempt must be made to help it should you follow the instructions on page 138 for reducing a dislocation.

Repeated Dislocations of the Shoulder

Approximately 90 percent of those under twenty-five who suffer anterior dislocations of the shoulder will be victims of a chronic condition that may require surgical correction. The only chance an injured person has of preventing this problem from becoming recurrent and disabling is to have it properly treated immediately. This means the shoulder must be immobilized for a period of six to eight weeks while the individual is under the care of a physician. This is only true of the first dislocation.

Unfortunately for those who experience repeated dislocations, the shoulder comes out more easily each time. Almost everyone knows of someone with a problem or trick shoulder that continues to go in and out. Once an athlete has had one true shoulder dislocation, treatment for subsequent dislocations consists simply of a sling for as long as the shoulder is sore. After a shoulder has become dislocated twice, subsequent dislocations are going to occur, and there is no point in subjecting a person in those circumstances to prolonged treatment that will probably be of little or no value. A person with a dislocating shoulder will be unable to throw overhand with the affected arm, or serve a tennis ball, or tackle anyone with the arm outstretched. Once a shoulder has started to dislocate easily, even putting an arm on the back of a car seat to turn around may cause it to go out.

If the shoulder only dislocates once a year, then it may not pay to have it repaired. However, if the dislocation prevents an activity that is considered valuable or it endangers life—if one must swim, for example—surgical repair is recommended. But expect some loss of motion in the shoulder after surgery. Usually, any loss of movement is limited and does not preclude activity in most sports, though the serving or throwing arm of a highly skilled player will probably not function as well as before the injury. The same holds true for certain gymnastic and swimming maneuvers.

Reducing a Forward Dislocation of the Shoulder

A forward dislocation of the shoulder can be gently remedied by a process called reducing. Almost without exception, this should only be attempted on someone who has already experienced at least one forward dislocation in the problem shoulder. Don't try to reduce a shoulder if you are afraid of doing so. The following description is a gentle, easy way to proceed, if you are willing to do so and the injured person will cooperate. Before starting, make sure that the athlete has had a previous forward dislocation and be sure the shoulder is similarly out of place.

1 / Have the person lie prostrate, face up.

2 / Tell the person to relax and cooperate; it's quite easy to reduce a dislocated shoulder in these circumstances.

3 / Firmly grasp the arm inside the elbow with one hand, holding the forearm in the other hand, and carefully lift the arm until it is

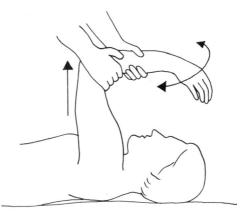

35 / Reducing an anterior (forward) shoulder dislocation. Someone who has already experienced an anterior shoulder dislocation can have any similar, subsequent dislocations corrected by a second party. To reduce a shoulder, have the person lie face up and relax completely. Lift the arm straight up in the air with one hand inside the elbow and the other hand on the forearm. While continuing to pull up on the arm, bend the elbow 90°, and then gently rock the forearm from side to side. The shoulder should slip back into place.

perpendicular to the ground. While continuing to pull up on the arm at the elbow, bend the elbow 90° and gently rock the forearm from side to side. If the person relaxes, this should be successful (Illustration 35).

If marked pain results from this attempt, the injured person is either tensed up and not able to cooperate, or there may be a fracture. In any case, at the sign of marked pain, stop, and transport the person to an emergency room.

Voluntary Dislocations of the Shoulder

Some people who never had a shoulder injury are able to dislocate a shoulder or both shoulders at will. Typically these people are quite flexible ("double-jointed"). They might delight in popping their shoulder in and out at a party simply to amuse the crowd, and they may be able to dislocate their shoulder in any direction. Voluntary dislocation of a shoulder should be discouraged however. Each dislocation can do a little harm to the joint surface, and with repeated dislocations and stretching of the tissues there is a risk of injuring the main nerves to the arm, causing pain or even partial paralysis of the limb. The best treatment for this condition is counseling and the discouragement of further dislocations. Unfortunately, surgery is obligatory at times due to pain from nerve injuries, but it generally ends in failure, with more pain and stiffness.

Shoulder "Slipping In and Out"

Another type of shoulder pain occurs in athletes who feel a shoulder start to go out and are then unable to do certain throwing, serving, hitting, gymnastic, or swimming maneuvers. These athletes feel a shoulder go in and out of place, but it is never dislocated so that someone else has to put it back in place.

This condition is frequently misdiagnosed and mistreated as tendinitis. It usually fails to respond to the varieties of medical treatment for tendinitis because it is, in fact, a mechanical abnormality that demands a mechanical solution. Generally, the pain is not disabling and does not last after the activity ceases (this is not typical of tendinitis).

Old-time surgeons say that if you listen to the patient long enough, they'll tell you the diagnosis. From years of practice, I, too, have learned that the patient is usually right. If I hear that a shoulder is going in and out, it may not be coming completely out, but chances are it is starting to go out, and the patient has been forced to stop an activity because of it.

Orthopedic thinking used to be that unless a shoulder was definitely dislocated, no surgery was indicated. With the advent of moving-picture X rays to help make or confirm a diagnosis, surgeons can now see a tendon snapping in and out of place or a shoulder actually starting to go out. Thus there is now a willingness among orthopedic surgeons to correct this problem surgically. If a true dislocation has not occurred, there is no need to strongly recommend surgical repair. And if the disability is only minor, or if it only prevents one activity, then the desirability of the sport must be weighed against the costs of an operation. If surgery is not worth it, there is little else that can be done to help strengthen the shoulder. Unfortunately, the person must just learn to put up with it.

Shoulder Pain in Throwing and Racket Sports

In adolescents under the age of sixteen, shoulder pain that is not associated with a specific injury in throwing or racket sports should be treated with ice and rest. This type of pain in youngsters is usually the result of muscle fatigue or failure to warm up properly. At that age there are very few chronic injuries in the shoulder that will not heal with adequate rest, ice, and a cessation of the offending activity until the pain is gone. Bluntly stated, a Little League player with a sore shoulder should simply not throw; he or she is throwing too much.

Adults who experience shoulder pain every time they throw, serve, or hit a ball in a racket sport are usually having a different problem entirely. For them the pain is generally the result of wear and tear and degeneration of the tendons, and the condition can become chronic if not cared for properly. In serious cases, the treatment is more difficult and the results are not as good as for young players because of the degenerative nature of the condition. At the onset of pain apply ice and rest the shoulder. Aspirin may also bring relief. To avoid worsening the condition, do not return to play until all pain has disappeared. Again, prevention is the best medicine.

Older teenagers may develop the true adult type of tendinitis in the shoulder, but this is not common. If the pain is very mild and it is localized, rest and the application of ice packs before and after the activity are the best treatment. The same treatment applies for the adult who has very mild symptoms. Such mild conditions are best remedied with adequate warm-ups, ice packs before and after playing, and an occasional aspirin. If this fails to relieve the problem, more complicated medical treatment will probably be necessary, on an elective basis. Unless the pain is acute, severe, and disabling, which would be uncommon in an athlete, an emergency room visit will not be fruitful.

Prevention of shoulder pain, tendinitis, and chronic strain in racket and throwing sports is clearly the best treatment, regardless of age. Recent evidence indicates that proper weight lifting as well as strengthening and flexibility exercises for the throwing arm are the key to preventing recurrent strain and resulting problems in the shoulder joint. Debate currently rages over the value of isokinetic versus isotonic exercise, but under a coach's direction either system will provide an effective means of strengthening the arms and shoulders.

Isokinetic machines have a distinct advantage over traditional weight lifting with barbells. They can be adjusted to correspond closely to a person's capacity, thus avoiding the pain and injury that could result from losing control of a heavy weight.

Chronic shoulder pain that occurs in throwing and racket sports is symptomatic of what is known in medical circles as overuse syndrome. In other words, to continue playing with a painful shoulder causes permanent damage that will become a chronic, disabling problem once it has gone too far. Prevention includes proper warm-ups and strengthening and conditioning exercises done ahead of time, and the avoidance of fatigue and overuse. Overuse is more common in adults than it is in young children, who frequently have the good sense to stop playing when something hurts.

Shoulder Pain in Swimmers

In modern swimming technique, the main power of the stroke comes from the upper extremities, or the shoulder girdle and arms. The old approach required a strong kick, but in modern competition swimming the legs do very little but keep the back half of the body afloat. As might be expected, the main problem of swimmers (other than breaststroker's knee) is shoulder pain.

As a general rule, most swimmers who see a physician about shoulder pain are told they have tendinitis and should quit swimming. Most likely this advice is ignored, and the patient continues to swim and complain of pain in the shoulder. Swimmers who seek two or three opinions and are still told the same thing tend to put up with the pain or find a physician who will give them cortisone injections, which may or may not help. Unfortunately, the medical literature describing shoulder pain in swimmers is extremely limited.

Shoulder pain in swimmers is different from shoulder pain in the fully grown, older athlete. In the adult over the age of twenty or twenty-five, bursitis or tendinitis in the shoulder usually causes restricted motion along with pain, but in swimmers there is virtually no restriction of motion. In fact, swimmers probably exhibit more mobility than the physician is used to seeing. Thus, if the pain is only mild and does not stop a swimmer from training or missing practice, the condition can probably be remedied personally. Only if it is difficult or impossible to practice or swim in meets should medical evaluation be necessary.

Treatment for pain in the shoulder of a swimmer varies according to the age of the person and the severity of the condition. For a swimmer under the age of twelve, it is best to stop swimming until the pain goes away. Unless a shoulder is being abused, shoulder pain is extremely rare in children of that age and should heal with rest. Constant pain that lasts for more than 24 hours following a complete rest of 48 to 72 hours should have medical attention because it could indicate a more serious problem. The presence of growth zones in the bones of adolescents will necessitate X rays to rule out any possibility of a fracture or other bone injury. I personally believe that if no lesions other than tendinitis are found in a child under twelve, rest, even if it takes several months, will heal almost every case. I would not use medication or injections for a child of that age.

For teenagers, treatment depends upon the physical maturity of the individual. Teenagers who are still growing are more appropriately treated like ten year olds, others should be handled as adults. Next, find out *when* the shoulder hurts and exactly *where* it hurts. Then, determine if the person has had a cold, a mild case of the flu, or mononucleosis.

Pain occurring in the area of the trapezius muscle (see Illustration 36), at the beginning or end of practice, is typical muscle pain that is probably benign. This condition is common among muscular swimmers who fail to warm up properly. These swimmers usually know when warm-ups are inadequate and can easily correct the problem.

Pain that starts near the end of practice, around the trapezius and deltoid muscles (see Illustration 36), is usually a sign of muscle fatigue. It means that a swimmer is out of condition or the workout is too strenuous. This type of pain generally shows up at the beginning of training and goes away as the season progresses.

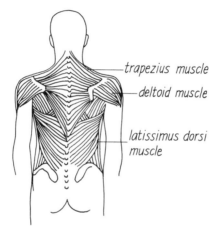

36/Back muscles important to throwing sports and swimming

A swimmer who has had a mild cold, a bout with the flu, or, particularly, a case of mononucleosis, will also experience the type of muscular shoulder pain associated with fatigue. In the recovery phase from a viral infection this kind of pain can be a very nagging problem. In addition to taking aspirin, there is little that can be done medically to speed recuperation. The understanding of a coach and parents will help during this difficult period. As long as there is no fever, workouts can resume.

Pain located at the front of the shoulder (Illustration 37) may be "swimmer's shoulder." In teenage competitive swimmers, this condition amounts to true tendinitis. It happens when blood flow to the tendons of the shoulder is decreased during one phase of the freestyle stroke in long distance swimming. This causes the tendons to become somewhat swollen and tender. The tendons may then push on the

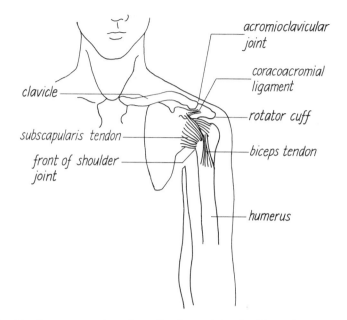

37/Shoulder ligaments and tendons. The front of the shoulder is the area most commonly involved in shoulder tendinitis and swimmer's shoulder. A major group of tendons associated with shoulder tendinitis is located in the region of the rotator cuff.

coracoacromial ligament or on the acromio process, which increases discomfort even more.

Swimmer's shoulder is most often found among distance free-stylers, butterfliers, and backstrokers, but it can also occur after a change in stroke mechanics or in competitive swimmers who do not swim nine to eleven months a year. With the distances demanded in modern training it is almost impossible for an older swimmer to train only four to six months a year and expect pain-free shoulders.

The best treatment for swimmer's shoulder is prevention. Modern weight-lifting techniques that provide proper strengthening of the shoulder, together with more reasonable training schedules, can elimi-nate much of the problem. A change in stroke or breathing patterns may help solve the situation as well. If mild shoulder pain persists in spite of these measures, the swimmer may have to be taken off dis-tance swimming until the pain disappears, and workouts may have to be altered. It is very safe to treat the shoulder with ice before and after practice. In the event that all of these measures fail and it becomes difficult or impossible to practice, or the swimmer misses a number of meets, medical evaluation is warranted, preferably by an orthopedic surgeon or a physician who is familiar with this type of problem. A physician unsympathetic to sports or not familiar with this condition will almost certainly diagnose tendinitis and recommend that swimming be discontinued. Of course, this will usually solve the problem, but it is not always acceptable to the patient.

An "apprehension shoulder" is one that is partially or incompletely dislocated (see page 139). This condition is common to swimmers, but if it becomes so disabling that a swimmer is unable to practice, surgery may be necessary. "Apprehension shoulder" is usually seen in backstrokers, especially when they touch the wall prior to making a turn. The shoulder will go out and come in by itself, causing pain and difficulty during the turn. Modification of the turn, if it can be done legally, is obviously the best solution. If this fails, orthopedic evaluation will be necessary.

Snapping Scapula or Shoulder Blade

A shoulder blade that pops or snaps as it glides along the back of the chest is called a snapping scapula. The condition is not serious and is best left untreated, unless accompanied by a definite, constant pain. If you do need medical attention and the doctor can actually show you a large bone spur or an abnormal bony projection on the shoulder blade, then and only then consider having surgery. After surgery, the shoulder blade can be expected to keep on snapping, but the pain will usually have lessened or disappeared. In cases where the X ray is normal, it is fruitless to have surgery since the snapping will probably continue. Before agreeing to surgery, get a second or even third opinion.

16 / Arms, Elbows, and Forearms

Arm Injuries in Children and Preteens

A CHILD or preteen who comes home cradling one arm in the other (Illustration 38) has probably suffered a fracture or dislocation at least until proved otherwise. The injury may be a fractured clavicle, humerus, or forearm, or a type of shoulder dislocation. In any case, that cradling posture is the one naturally assumed by people who have an injury in the arm or shoulder; it's extremely unlikely that a youngster would fake it. Any child complaining of pain in the upper arm must be treated on the assumption that the arm is fractured, even if there is no deformity and the child can move the arm fairly well. Minor fractures may show little or no deformity, minimal swelling, and pain only on certain movements.

Many children suffer so-called buckle fractures (medically known as torus fractures) in which the bone is slightly buckled or crinkled. Buckle fractures are quite stable and happen only to the immature bones of children. With simple immobilization such fractures will heal in a matter of a few weeks.

Provided the appearance of the injury is not alarming, there is no marked swelling, and only moderate pain that does not extend into the elbow or lower arm, it is reasonable to ice down the arm, apply a sling, and wait for twenty-four hours. Persistent pain at this stage indicates the need for a medical evaluation. If an appointment with a doctor cannot be made soon, take the child to an emergency room for an X-ray evaluation.

A severe-looking injury accompanied by swelling or marked pain, or any pain in the elbow, needs immediate medical attention.

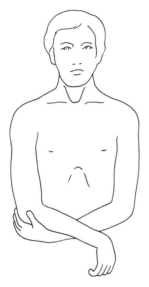

38/Typical position of person with shoulder or arm injury. People who suffer shoulder or arm injuries find this position to be the most comfortable for supporting the arm on the way to the doctor or emergency room.

Pain in the Upper Arm

Any athlete who complains of an injury between the shoulder and elbow, especially while cradling the arm (Illustration 38), probably has a fracture.

Arm injuries complicated by marked swelling and pain indicate muscle ruptures or bone fractures, even if the arm can be moved. While muscle ruptures are rare in individuals under twenty-five, the biceps of older people can rupture as the result of a violent pull. The injured person usually "knows" muscles were torn and experiences both pain and some swelling. In most cases, the treatment is surgical repair, although it is not mandatory. A rupture will usually heal naturally, but leaves some weakness and deformity in the muscle. Use ice and a sling for first aid. Consultation should be sought within twenty-four hours.

An adult who has fallen on an arm and is unable to move it usually knows if it is out of place or fractured. If the arm moves abnormally, it is fractured. Treat with a sling, ice, and a trip to an emergency room if you can't contact your physician.

Swelling and pain from repeated blows to the arm can lead to hemorrhaging in the muscle with resulting calcification and the formation of bone. This condition is called myositis ossificans. If an injury resulted from repeated blows it is wise to inform the physician of that fact. Without this information, the calcium or early bone formation resulting from trauma can be mistaken for a bone tumor. Normal treatment is rest from sporting activity, ranging from a week to a few months.

Elbow Injuries

As an absolute rule, any injury to the elbow that brings moderate to severe pain and swelling, whether or not there is deformity, must have medical consultation. Any injury with marked pain or swelling demands emergency consultation. This includes a dislocated elbow. Do not pull on the deformed or swollen elbow of an injured person; the risk of causing more damage is much greater than any benefit that could be derived.

Orthopedic surgeons especially fear elbow injuries in children because they are usually accompanied by profound swelling and most of the complications of a fracture sometimes occur there. In other words, elbow injuries are never to be taken lightly.

Medical treatment may include a splint, a cast, or even, for children, surgery or weeks in traction. If not treated in a splint or cast, certain types of dislocations may lead to other troubles. This is especially true in regard to athletes who are very flexible or double-jointed.

One common complication of elbow dislocations is myositis ossificans, caused by bleeding into the muscles that leads to calcium deposits and the formation of abnormal bone.

A typical example was a fourteen-year-old boy who was brought to me with a stiff elbow that reduced his arm movement by half. His X rays revealed a large bone deposit in front of the elbow, so I asked his mother when the elbow had been dislocated. She denied the boy had ever injured it. But when I asked him about it, he replied, "Oh, four weeks ago I fell at football practice and the coach put my elbow back in place." Apparently the mother had never been notified, and the boy never told her about the injury for fear of having to drop out of football practice. The fact that the arm had not been immobilized may very well have aggravated the problem, although the complication might have occurred regardless. The coach certainly did not do the boy a favor because it took approximately six months for the elbow to heal. Again, a dislocated elbow must receive proper treatment; it should not be attempted by a layman, except possibly under extreme circumstances in the wilderness.

If a child experiences swelling around the elbow, but is able to move the arm and there seems to be no significant injury, find out what happened. It may have been a fall resulting in severe pain at the time of the accident. It would then be wise to ask if anyone else touched the elbow or pulled it back into place. If so, find out if the pain lessened. A positive answer probably means the elbow was dislocated. Treat the swelling with ice, apply a sling, and seek consultation with a physician or an orthopedic surgeon within twenty-four hours.

Occasionally, an injury to the inner side of the elbow in a child or growing adolescent gives localized pain and swelling (Illustration 39).

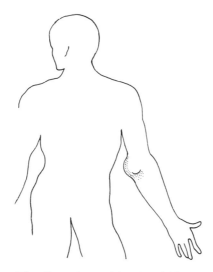

39/Pull-off fracture at the elbow. An arm injury in a child or still-developing adolescent may result in a pull-off fracture of a growth zone (apophysis) on the inner side of the elbow. This happens when a tendon or ligament is stronger than the bone to which it is connected. The reflex of such tissue during an accident may actually pull-off, or fracture, a bone, resulting in swelling, bruising, and pain.

If the elbow can be moved back and forth and bent without difficulty, medical attention can be put off for twenty-four hours, as long as ice is applied and a sling is used. This is probably a fracture, and X rays must be taken because such injuries sometimes require surgery. Never ignore this condition or treat it lightly.

A minor type of elbow injury is olecranon bursitis, or beer-drinker's bursitis (Illustration 40). It frequently occurs from a blow to the tip of the elbow. This may cause hemorrhaging into the bursa, a small, fluid-filled sac located in the loose skin behind the elbow, or irritation that will make the bursa fill with additional fluid. In most cases, there is virtually no pain, only marked swelling and discoloration that can frighten a parent. While the condition is also a bit disconcerting to the athlete as well, it is not a real problem.

This injury is particularly common in athletes who play on artificial surfaces. They should wear protective pads over areas that are likely to be hit in a fall. Football and possibly even soccer players should always wear elbow pads to prevent this problem.

If the swelling is only mild or moderate, ice and an elastic bandage are adequate treatment. In cases of extreme swelling, a physician may need to draw excess fluid from the bursa.

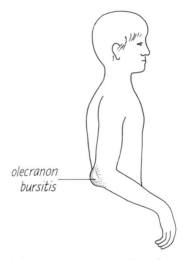

olecranon bursitis

40/Olecranon bursitis. Blows on the tip of the elbow frequently result in olecranon, or beer-drinker's, bursitis. The bursitis is caused by hemorrhaging into a small, fluid-filled sac (bursa) in the loose skin of the elbow, or by irritation that brings additional fluid into the sac. This injury is common among athletes who play on artificial surfaces.

Little League Elbow

Little League elbow can involve a complicated orthopedic injury to the bones of the joint, although it is occasionally a simple problem. In any case, all throwing should be stopped at the onset of pain, and medical care should be received before throwing is resumed.

Little League elbow has given the game a bad name, but it is not a common injury. While some people may think the condition only shows up in pitchers, it can really occur to any player who throws the ball a lot, such as the shortstop, catcher, or first baseman.

If your Little Leaguer comes home complaining of elbow pain, there are two things to do: First, look at the elbow and find out where it hurts. If there is no deformity or swelling, then have the youngster stand in front of you with arms outstretched. If the elbows straighten out similarly on both sides, there probably is no cause for concern. But if one elbow is at least 15 degrees less than fully straight, something may be wrong with it and an orthopedic examination and X rays are necessary. I strongly believe that any child who lacks full extension of the elbow should not throw from any position on the field before undergoing a medical examination.

Pulled Elbow in a Child Under Six

Because it only occurs in children between the ages of one and five, a pulled elbow really isn't an athletic injury, but it does happen sometimes when small children are being tossed around to amuse them. The technical term for this injury (also known as nursemaid's elbow) is subluxed radial head. It is caused by a forceful jerk or pull on the child's elbow. This will partially pull the upper end of the radius out of joint. (The radius is the large bone of the lower arm.) When this happens, the child instantly shrieks in pain and acts as though the arm has been paralyzed. Physicians sometimes mistake this condition for paralysis or a severe dislocation of the shoulder and/or elbow, particularly if they are not experienced in children's problems.

It is best to seek medical advice for this injury. Often the pain is so severe that the child should be taken directly to an emergency room. If you are far from medical treatment and certain that the injury occurred from a forceful jerk on the child's arm, then gently examine the arm. In a gentle manner and without moving the wrist, make sure that the shoulder and wrist are not tender by pressing them lightly. If all the pain seems to be in the elbow, reassure the child and gently hold his or her elbow in one hand, with the elbow bent at about ninety degrees from the ground. Then carefully grasp the child's hand, putting your thumb in the palm, and quickly turn the hand palm up. If the injury is a pulled elbow, you will feel a click and hear a loud scream, but the recovery will be almost instantaneous. If that fails, you must seek medical care, even though it is hours away.

Elbow Pain in Teenagers and Adults

In sports, the main stress to an elbow usually comes from serious throwing or the serving of a tennis ball. Actually, the biomechanics of both motions are the same.

The movement puts tremendous pressure on the elbow, principally on the inner (medial) side, but also along the outer joint surface. Over years of repetitive throwing, the joint may become damaged, resulting in loose bone chips and eventually arthritis (Illustration 41). The throwing will also stretch out the ligaments. As a result, it is common for the

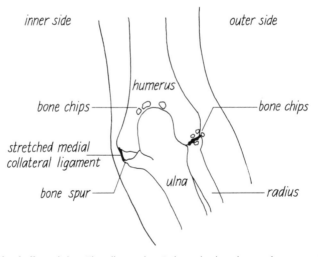

41/Back of elbow joint. The elbow of a pitcher who has thrown for years, despite a sore elbow, is usually marked by stretched ligaments, bone chips and bone spurs at the joint, and a shortening of the radius from wearing down.

bone to actually become worn down so that the elbow is physically shortened. Some famous pitchers retired when they noted that their pitching arm was becoming shorter than the other one. This is not imaginary, but the reward of throwing at a professional level for many years. A sore elbow in pitchers is a real problem. Minor pains can be safely treated with ice, but the minute an athlete loses full extension of the arm, thorough orthopedic evaluation with X rays is necessary.

Tennis Elbow

Most elbow pain in the young, high caliber tennis player or in players under 25 occurs on the inner side of the elbow and is really related to the sore elbow condition experienced by a pitcher and just described.

True tennis elbow applies principally to adults over the age of 25 who have developed pain in the outer, or lateral, aspect of the elbow; that is, in the area of the bony prominence at the end of the upper arm near the elbow joint. Any pain in this region (Illustration 42) is a sign of tennis elbow. Beginning and average adult tennis players suffer this problem the most, but it is occasionally found in an excellent young player who grossly abuses the elbow.

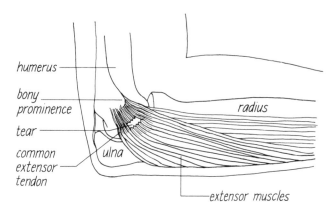

42/Tennis elbow. Small tears in the extensor tendon, which links the extensor muscles to the bony prominence at the end of the humerus, are the most common cause of tennis elbow. Beginning and intermediate adult players over the age of twenty-five are the principle victims of this affliction.

Small tears in the common extensor tendon are generally thought to be the cause of tennis elbow. This tendon connects most of the muscles that open up the fingers and pull up the wrist. It is also connected to the outer part of the elbow joint.

The usual cause of tennis elbow is an incorrectly hit backhand. But before the current tennis boom, politicians, carpenters, and electricians were the most common sufferers of this affliction that also results from excessive hand-shaking, nail-pounding, or turning of a screwdriver. The worst case that I ever saw was that of a commodity broker who developed it from continuously shaking his hand on the floor of the exchange.

Good form is the best insurance against tennis elbow, with proper conditioning a close second. The hardest cases of this problem to treat occur in nonathletic women over the age of thirty who suddenly take up tennis. What they do, of course, is pick up a heavy racket and begin hitting the ball incorrectly and repetitively. Eventually, this causes tears in the common extensor tendon, resulting in inflammation and pain. If ignored, this condition will lead to recurring disability during play, and it may become so frustrating that it will turn a player from the sport.

To prevent tennis elbow from developing, beginners should take tennis lessons. I should also mention that tennis elbow is virtually unknown in two-handed backhanders, regardless of their skill level. Most pros are scandalized by this statement and some virtually refuse to teach this method of hitting a backhand, even though a number of top-ranking players have proved it to be extremely effective. But if you have a mild case of tennis elbow, it might be worth your while to insist on learning the two-handed backhand, even though the pro may insist that your elbow won't suffer if you hit the backhand properly with one hand.

Tennis elbow has been widely studied by the medical profession because so many tennis-playing doctors have been afflicted with the problem. But, in spite of all the research that has been done, the basic facts remain the same. The condition can be prevented and helped by proper muscle-strengthening exercises.

A classic exercise is repetitive squeezing of a tennis ball, a piece of clay, or a special wrist-strengthening device. All of these are effective, since strong forearm muscles lessen vulnerability to tennis elbow. It goes without saying, that no exercise should be done in the presence of pain.

Minor cases of tennis elbow can be treated effectively with ice packs and aspirin. A special tennis elbow-band that spreads out the muscle pull will also provide some relief.

When pain is mild to moderate, limited to the outer part of the elbow, and only occurs while playing tennis, shaking hands, or doing a similar activity, medical attention is probably not necessary. This is especially true for someone who is unwilling to take medication or recoils at the thought of a cortisone injection in the tender area.

I believe that tennis elbow is one of those medical conditions for which a patient can basically choose the treatment. For severe pain, however, it is best to see a physician who can administer a cortisone injection. If you do seek medical consultation, expect X rays to be ordered, since a full evaluation will probably be necessary. Certainly any injury associated with a specific episode or one that shows any swelling requires a medical evaluation. The problem may not be tennis elbow. Surgery is the court of last resort (pardon the pun) for tennis elbow, but it should only be performed in those cases where the elbow has failed to respond to cortisone injections. Surgery helps to reduce the pain and disability, but does not guarantee complete relief. Recovery may require a few weeks in a cast and several months of graduated exercises to achieve normal flexibility and strength.

You may have noticed in the suggested treatment for tennis elbow that I neglected to mention rest, the sine qua non for curing most forms of tendinitis. That was deliberate. Most people are either unwilling to rest a tennis elbow or have tried and, out of frustration and a desire to resume the game, have given that up as a viable alternative.

As tough as it is to admit or like it, tennis elbow should be considered a condition of middle age, at least according to some hard-hearted authorities on the subject, myself included. After the elbow has received a certain amount of abuse, it may fail to respond to all conservative treatment, so many people simply decide to put up with the condition. This alternative is not painless, but it is safe.

Occasionally an excellent tennis player develops tennis elbow. For example, a top player might practice a thousand serves in an afternoon, go on to play five to seven sets of vigorous tennis, and then, in spite of elbow pain, play two or three more sets. That is flagrant abuse of the elbow, and the tears resulting in the tendon are clearly due to muscle fatigue and an overriding lack of common sense.

Tennis elbow is also seen in high-level tennis players who put a great deal of top spin on their forehands, or try an exaggerated American twist serve. In any case, the treatment for tennis elbow remains the same.

Forearm Problems

Pain in the forearm is not a common athletic problem, except in male gymnasts and excluding any pain that may be associated with tennis elbow. Gymnastics require weight bearing and heavy pulling, lifting, and swinging on the forearms. Unfortunately there is a paucity of medical literature on this condition, but it is probably the upper-extremity equivalent of shin splints in the legs. If rest and the ministrations of a trainer do not prove adequate treatment, medical evaluation is necessary. If a fracture of the forearm occurs, it will probably be accompanied by disability and often a marked deformity or swelling. In such cases, emergency-room treatment is warranted.

Funny Bone

The funny bone is neither funny nor a bone. It is the ulnar nerve, which controls most of the small muscles in the hand and gives sensation to the little finger and half of the ring finger. This nerve can be felt in the groove between the two bony points on the inner side of the elbow. Leaning on this area, a blow to it or any type of pressure will cause numbness and tingling in both the little finger and ring finger. A hard blow can cause a painful electric sensation in the fingers. Bicycle racers are frequently troubled by irritation to this nerve resulting from leaning on the handlebars with bent elbows.

Irritation of the ulnar nerve is usually minor and short-lived. For the most part, ice applied to the injured area and protection from further pressure are all the treatment needed. But if there is numbness that lasts for more than a few seconds, the problem is likely to be serious and medical evaluation is recommended.

17 / Wrists, Hands, and Fingers

Wrist Injuries

ANY child who has fallen hard on the wrist may have a minor fracture, even if the wrist and fingers can be moved normally, no marked deformity is evident, and there is little swelling. If the child is still growing, or it is a boy under sixteen or a girl under fourteen, tenderness when the wrist is grasped probably indicates a fracture. (See "How to Evaluate an Injury," page 51.)

In children, a torus, or buckle, fracture commonly occurs at the lower end of the radius near the wrist. This type of fracture is similar to a crinkle in the bone, but it is usually very stable and can be treated with a short cast for approximately three to four weeks. If there is no marked deformity or swelling and only minimal pain, it is safe to apply ice and a sling for a day to see if the pain persists. At that stage, if there is still pain when a person gently grabs the forearm near the wrist, X-ray evaluation by a physician is warranted, since a minor torus fracture or minor fracture through the growth plate is probably present.

In cases where an individual complains of a sprained wrist but there is no deformity and only mild to moderate pain, it is wise to locate the swelling and tenderness. If there is tenderness around the bone at the inner side of the wrist, as in Illustration 43, then a serious fracture of the navicular could be present, and a doctor should be seen within twenty-four to forty-eight hours. Meanwhile, treat the injury with ice.

The navicular is an essential small bone in the wrist joint that is a notoriously slow healer. On the average, it takes a minimum of four to six months to mend. If it is not treated intensively with a plaster cast, preferably within the first few weeks of injury, it may never heal, and

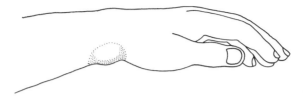

43/Fractured wrist joint. Swelling or tenderness around the navicular bone, indicated in the shaded area, represents a serious fracture in the wrist joint. Never assume that these symptoms represent a sprained wrist, as sprained wrists almost never occur.

may wear more on the joint, leading to significant arthritis in that area.

It is probably safe to say that a sprained wrist cannot be properly diagnosed without X rays. Many injuries that have been called sprained wrists have, in fact, been navicular fractures. The medical pitfall is that even the best of X rays taken on initial examination can appear normal although a fracture is present. Whenever a wrist injury in the area just described is persistently tender, it is wise to have a second set of X rays made two weeks after the injury. These new X rays often show a fracture that may not have been visible at the time of the accident. It is mandatory that this type of problem be evaluated medically. A physician who recommends follow-up X rays in two weeks is providing good treatment.

Fractures of this type are popularly called Joe Namath or Bobby Douglas fractures, since both of these famous NFL quarterbacks had them. Joe Namath was forced to miss half a season because of his mishap. I think that if the New York Jets were willing to permit the absence of their star player for a season, you deserve no less. The risks of serious complications are too high to treat this injury lightly.

Other Wrist Injuries

In the preceding discussion I have stressed that any exceptionally painful, or swollen, or deformed wrist condition requires prompt medical attention. If there is numbness in the thumb or fingers, emergency treatment is absolutely necessary. But in cases where there is only mild to moderate pain and swelling and the hour is inconvenient, ice and splinting provide adequate treatment for twenty-four hours, or until it is possible to see a doctor or go to an emergency room.

Injuries to the Thumb

Any injury that causes marked swelling, pain, or tenderness at the base of the thumb (Illustration 44) may represent a Bennetts fracture and should receive immediate medical care. These potentially disabling fractures frequently require surgery and should not be ignored or slighted. It is virtually impossible to tell the severity of this type of fracture without X rays. In cases where there is only mild to moderate discomfort with normal sensation in the fingers and thumb, evaluation can wait twenty-four hours if ice packs are applied and the hand is kept elevated.

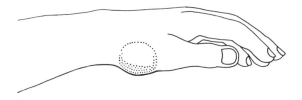

44/Fractured thumb. Swelling, bruising, or tenderness in the area around the base of the thumb probably represents a serious fracture.

Another common, very severe injury to the thumb occurs just above its base, particularly to skiers who fall and catch the thumb in the loop of a ski pole. It can also happen when the thumb gets caught in a jersey or piece of equipment and is pulled hard. This condition is often called gamekeeper's thumb because English gamekeepers often developed it from killing rabbits by hand. These injuries of the thumb can be quite

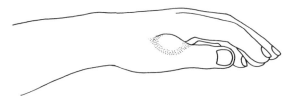

45/Gamekeeper's thumb. Swelling and tenderness on the inner side of the thumb, just above the base, may represent a severe ligament injury, especially if it is impossible to pinch with strength.

devastating. If there is tenderness along the inner side of the thumb (Illustration 45) and the person is unable to pinch or resist pressure, then at least a plaster cast is needed, even if X rays appear normal. Occasionally this type of injury will also require surgery. Improper treatment may lead to a loss of the ability to pinch with resistance, and a permanently weakened thumb. Any severe injury to the thumb deserves full care. Ice packs and elevation of the hand are good first aid, but medical attention should be sought between twenty-four and forty-eight hours after the injury, if pain and weakness in the thumb persist.

Injuries to the Fingers

Most knuckle injuries result from an intentional blow that was delivered to someone's jaw, a wall, a helmet, or another hard object. Assume that any hand with swollen or bruised knuckles (see Illustration 46) has a boxer's fracture, until proved otherwise. Generally, this type of fracture is not an emergency and can be treated overnight with ice and elevation. But X-ray evaluation is necessary because the swelling is usually so extreme that it would conceal a deformity. While most of these fractures require only simple treatment, those with severe deformations may very well demand setting or even surgery.

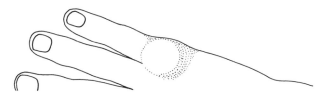

46/Boxer's fracture. A swollen and bruised knuckle, resulting from an intentional blow of the fist, is the sign of a boxer's fracture. This type of injury can occur to any finger and requires attention.

Other fractures sometimes occur further down the hand if it is stepped on or receives a strong blow of some kind. Basically, any extremely swollen and tender hand deserves X-ray evaluation within twenty-four to seventy-two hours, even if one can use it. Prior to seeing a doctor treat the hand with ice and keep it elevated.

A third common sports injury to the hand is baseball finger, some-times referred to as mallet finger. If a player complains of an injured finger and the finger is bent in an abnormal direction, medical attention is necessary.

This type of injury occurs most often from catching a large or fast ball on the tip of a finger. The ball forcefully bends the finger down, causing a tendon to rupture or the bone to break. If the finger can no longer be straightened completely, especially at the last joint, the injury has probably torn the extensor tendon which straightens the finger. Because it is virtually impossible to tell the difference between a tendon rupture and a bone fracture without X rays, I believe they should be made any time a finger cannot be fully straightened at the tip (Illustration 47). These injuries are serious and often require six to eight weeks of splinting, even if no fracture is present. In fact, small fractures frequently heal better than tendon ruptures, but, occasion-ally, surgery may be necessary.

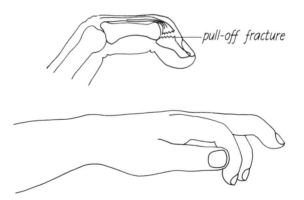

pull-off fracture

47/Baseball finger. The forceful bending down of a finger, often caused by catching a large or fast ball at the fingertip, may rupture an extensor tendon or fracture a finger bone. This tendon keeps the finger straight, so an inability to straighten or bend the finger indicates a definite problem.

If the injured finger cannot be bent at the tip, the flexor tendon on the palm side of the finger is probably ruptured and function can only be restored with surgery, preferably within the first seven to ten days, and by a specialist.

This type of injury should never be neglected or left untreated to suit one's convenience, or until the end of a playing season. Postponement of medical attention may lead to permanent loss of the ability to straighten or bend the finger, since neither of these functions is self-correcting. Ignoring a bone fracture or a fracture-dislocation may result in a painful arthritic condition.

Dislocated Fingers

There are two basic types of finger dislocation. The first kind is not common and can occur to any finger where it joins the hand. *Never* pull on a dislocated finger or thumb of this sort because the chances of putting it back in place are very slim. In most cases, surgery is required to correct the dislocation. No matter where such an accident happens, X rays are necessary.

The other kind of dislocation involves the middle joint of the finger. This is a common injury in many sports. It is sometimes called "coach's finger," probably because more coaches than physicians have treated the condition. Very likely it is also the cause of most painful, swollen joints in ex-athletes. If a finger ever becomes dislocated, X rays are mandatory to rule out the possibility of a fracture, even if a friend or coach puts it back in place.

I know that during one nationally televised NFL game, a player apparently sustained a dislocated finger and had it treated by a fellow player in full view of the TV cameras. This is not appropriate or standard care, and should never be applied to children. If you, your friend, or your child has sustained a dislocated finger and you are reasonably close to a hopsital, you should go there for X rays and medical attention, or see a doctor within several hours.

If medical attention is hours away, as in the wilderness, then giving the finger one quick, firm pull will probably not do any harm. If it goes back into place, a great service will have been rendered. But the finger should still be X-rayed because certain fractures commonly associated with a dislocated finger may be present and may eventually cause loss of function. Obviously there are times a person can get away with no medical treatment, but to lose the use of a finger because you guessed wrong doesn't make sense.

When a child complains of having injured a finger, review the above. It will prevent the kind of mistreatment that so frequently occurs in finger injuries. Ask if the finger was dislocated. An injured person will usually know the answer. If the response is affirmative, then ask if someone pulled on it. If the answer is again yes, arrange for a medical examination, including X rays, within the next day or two.

When a finger dislocation does not seem to have occurred and there is no marked swelling or deformity, ask the child to straighten out the finger. Be sure every joint is extended and then make certain that the finger, including the tip, can be bent. If so you can probably assume that the injury is minor and no medical care is warranted. However, if the thumb shows marked bruising and swelling, especially in any of the areas pictured in Illustrations 44 through 47, it is wise to seek medical evaluation within twenty-four to forty-eight hours. In the meantime treat the injury with ice and keep the hand elevated.

Injury to the Nail

One of the most painful accidents is a crushing or pounding injury to the nailbed of a finger. Mild to moderate pain with no marked discoloration under the nail can usually be treated with only ice and aspirin, but any open laceration should have emergency medical care.

When pain is marked and most of the nail is discolored, the tip of the finger is probably fractured (Illustration 48). Generally, the fracture is not major, but the collection of blood under the nail can be very painful and, over a period of hours, a pounding, throbbing, severe pain can develop. A physician can very easily relieve the pressure caused by the blood under the nail by drilling a small hole through the nail. Although this may sound frightening, the procedure is surprisingly painless and effective, and it can be done either in a doctor's office or emergency room. These injuries frequently result in loss of the nail, but it should grow back in approximately three months.

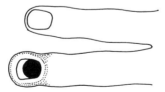

48/Bruised or crushed finger. Typically, a painful collection of blood will gather under the nail of a badly bruised or crushed fingertip.

18 / Skin

Sunburn

SUNBURN is the skin's reaction to the burning rays of sunlight. The burn actually begins to appear two to eight hours after exposure, depending on how intense the sun is. Maximum redness and pain in the skin will occur in twelve hours and begin to subside in three to four days.

The best treatment for sunburn is protection. Swimming usually offers no protection whatsoever. In fact, the cooling effect of water will sometimes hide any burning sensation. It is estimated that unless one swims more than three feet below the surface, water is no barrier to the sun's rays. Foggy and cloudy days do shield the sun somewhat, but when it is cooler people tend to stay out longer. And even on hazy days, ultraviolet rays still cause sunburn. This accounts for the fact that sunburn frequently seems worse on those days.

Any reaction to the sun that results in redness and pain is a first degree sunburn. Blisters form in a second degree burn. When a second degree burn covers more than 25 percent of the body, a physician should be consulted. One remedy that may cut down the painful reaction and burning effect is to take twice the normal dose of aspirin as soon as you *think* you may have a burn. Four hours later, take another double dose. After that, take only the standard recommended dose for a couple of days to keep down the inflammation.

Another treatment for sunburn is a mixture of crushed ice, one part bath oil, and five parts of water. Use this as a compress on the burned areas. Cooling the skin a few degrees will cut down on the chemical reaction of the burn if treatment is started soon enough.

The most obvious protective measure against the sun is clothing. To see if an article of clothing provides adequate shielding, hold it up to the sun and see how much light filters through it.

Sunscreen compounds are helpful too. They should, of course, be put on before, not after, exposure to the sun. The one most widely prescribed by dermatologists and readily available in drugstores is a 5 percent solution of PABA (para-amino-benzoic acid). *Caution:* Two percent of the population is allergic to this compound, so if any itching or redness develops, discontinue its use.

Sensitivity to sunburn is not related to eye color at all, but to skin, of which there are four basic types. These are: 1) skin that burns but never tans; 2) skin that burns but retains small amounts of tan; 3) skin that burns slightly and develops a good tan; and 4) skin that rarely burns and always tans. Although the first three skin types are the most sensitive to sunburn, the fourth can also be endangered by prolonged exposure.

Frostbite

Frostbite occurs when tissues are exposed to the cold for long periods of time. The severity of damage varies with both temperature and length of exposure. Freezing begins when the temperature in the deepest parts of tissues reaches ten degrees Celsius (40°F). The lowest temperature to which cells may be frozen and still survive is minus five degrees Celsius (23°F). Frostbite usually occurs from exposure over a period of several hours.

First-degree frostbite consists of swelling and redness in the affected part without any permanent damage. Second-degree frostbite is marked by the formation of blisters. In the third-degree stage, the skin dies and frequently turns black. By the fourth and last degree of frostbite, the affected part becomes gangrenous, requiring eventual amputation. Any frostbite beyond the first degree should be treated by a physician.

The first indication of frostbite is whiteness of the skin on the nose, earlobes, fingertips or toes. The affected part will feel frozen or doughy, and if the whiteness does not turn red with pressure, frostbite is progressing. If possible, start the following treatment:

1/ Remove the affected part from the wind.

2/ Treat the injured part *gently.* Don't make matters worse by rubbing, and do not apply snow or rub with ice. Rubbing will only make matters worse, and snow or ice will just add more chill to the skin.

3/ Do not put anything tight over the frostbitten area, and try to warm it up as quickly as possible without going to extremes. Fingertips can be warmed in the armpit. The tip of the nose or earlobes can be cupped in a hand, and toes and fingertips can be warmed somewhat by blowing on them. Be careful, though, that a hand does not become frostbitten while treating another area.

If frostbite is feared, get out of the cold and immediately begin soaking the affected area in warm water. But if a whole arm or leg is involved, the warming should be done in a hospital. The proper water temperature for this is between 37.7 degrees Celsius (100°F) and 40.6 degrees Celsius (105°F). Never guess at the warmth of the water: if it is higher than 40.6 degrees Celsius (105°F) it may be harmful; if lower, it may not help much. You must use a thermometer and maintain an even level of heat. Don't forget that the cold hand or foot will make the water cool off, and don't stop treatment if blisters appear, since they may be a favorable sign.

Prevention is the rule. Always pay attention to the windchill factor, which is often announced in weather broadcasts. Windchill affects exposed skin, but it should be considered even if you think you are wearing enough clothing. If frost begins to form on a sweatsuit or the suit starts to freeze, it's a good indication you are starting to get too cold.

Other factors that sometimes influence the athlete in cold weather are tight clothing, immobility, and sweating. Tight clothing predisposes the wearer to frostbite because it loses heat faster than loose clothing, and immobility is bad because the body produces less heat when it is inactive. Also remember that the combination of windchill and damp, sweaty clothing can be devastating. It is especially important to keep children in clothes that will stay dry.

Cold weather itself should not preclude outdoor activity. It cannot really injure the lungs, though breathing when it is very cold sometimes feels painful. Common sense and appropriate dress are necessary. For strenuous exercise, a light nylon jacket gives ideal wind protection and will not impede most exercising.

Chafing

Chafing is repeated rubbing of the skin that causes redness, soreness, and even blisters, if ignored. The prevention and the treatment for this condition are the same: Vaseline. Of course, smooth clothing also helps. Band-Aids prevent or protect sore nipples in runners.

Blisters

Blisters are usually the result of a continuous rubbing against the skin. The best treatment is obviously prevention. It used to be common practice to buy gym shoes a half size to a full size too big and then fill them by wearing two or three pairs of socks to prevent blisters. But a properly fitted shoe is really best. The number and type of socks are an individual matter; some runners never wear socks.

For blisters on the feet, wash the foot with a good unperfumed soap, such as Ivory. Then dry the foot and apply an antiseptic solution, such as Betadine Solution, which will burn slightly, to help cleanse the feet of bacteria. Cover the blister with a Band-Aid and wear white socks until the blister has healed; the dye in some colored socks can be irritating or harmful. Until the blister has healed, repeat this treatment twice a day. At night, remove the bandage and leave the blister uncovered.

Blisters on the hand require different care. First wash and dry the blister and then apply Vaseline. This treatment will usually permit resumption of an activity, unless it involves constant use of the hand. For added comfort, a bandage may be applied over the Vaseline.

Abrasions, or Floorburns

Abrasions can be very nasty wounds. The worst occur in skateboarding, motorcycling, and on artificial playing surfaces. Treat the abrasion by washing it with a gentle soap and water to remove any dirt and grass. Then continue to keep it clean by washing it twice a day. In addition, keep the wound as exposed to the air as possible for speedy healing.

If fluid oozes from the abrasion, give the wound a gentle painting with an antiseptic solution, such as Betadine, and then cover it with a dry dressing. Within a few hours, the dressing will stick to the wound, but pulling it off gently, even if it causes some bleeding, will promote healing by helping to remove dead tissue from the abrasion.

Medical attention is required if any material is so deeply embedded in the skin that you can't remove it. Asphalt is particularly difficult to extract from skin and can become a permanent tattoo if left in a wound. These are difficult, nasty injuries to treat, and the thought of them makes me cringe everytime I see someone barefoot or in shorts on a motorcycle.

If an abrasion reaches a bone, tendon, joint, or the layer of fat beneath the skin, seek medical attention. Marked swelling, especially over the elbow or knee, or the removal of a whole thickness of skin in either of these areas also requires medical care.

Cuts, or Lacerations

It is difficult to give hard-and-fast rules for treating cuts, but here are a few guidelines. Any cut accompanied by marked bleeding should be medically evaluated. Pressure directly on the wound will stop any bleeding and can be applied with a finger, a clean towel, or, ideally, a sterile dressing. *Never use a tourniquet to stop bleeding!* A surgeon will put a finger on a bleeding spot to stop the flow of blood during surgery. Old-fashioned first aid books have charts that map out points where the application of pressure supposedly stops bleeding, but these systems don't work very well. The only pressure point you need to know is the one that is actually bleeding.

Most cuts will heal even if they are not sutured, or stitched. But sutures promote healing, decrease the width of a scar, and improve appearance. Some cuts may take several weeks to heal and may be a bit messy for a week or two if not treated medically. As a rule, any gaping cut should probably be stitched, and any deep cut over a joint or on the hand or the foot should be seen by a doctor. To avoid cosmetically unacceptable results, it is also best to suture even a small cut on the edge of the lip, eyelid, or eyebrow. Also, cuts on the head that bleed a lot are frequently stitched to stop the bleeding.

To treat a cut, wash it gently with an unperfumed soap and then use "butterfly" tapes or a Band-Aid to pull the edges of the cut together. Healing time varies, depending on where a cut is located: head and face, three to five days; arm and leg, ten to fourteen days; foot, about fourteen days.

Tetanus

Once an adult or child has been immunized against tetanus, it is almost impossible to contract. Tetanus boosters are only needed every five years or so, after a person has had the first series of immunizations as a child. If you have been immunized, only deep, extensive, dirty wounds that would require medical care anyway may require a booster. If for any reason you were never immunized, then any time the skin is broken, regardless of the size or type of wound, seek medical treatment within twenty-four hours and inform the doctor that you were never immunized.

Human Bites

Infections can occur from human bites because the bacteria in the mouth are usually quite dangerous anywhere else in the body. In sports, human bites are most often caused inadvertently during a fight, when a punch is delivered to the mouth. Any time a human bite completely breaks the skin, it should have medical attention. It is safe to wash the bite with soap or an antiseptic solution, but do seek care as well.

Dog Bites

Fortunately, the dreaded disease of rabies is quite rare. Anyone bitten by a dog should first locate and identify the dog. If it is healthy, has been vaccinated against rabies, and lives for two weeks after the bite occurred, the chances of rabies are nil. But any deep dog bite should be medically evaluated, because it can cause serious infection, especially when located in the hand or foot. If the bite is really only a scratch, and there is no chance of rabies or tetanus, medical care is probably not warranted.

Since prevention is the best medicine, here are a few tips for avoiding dog bites. Dogs are a problem primarily for joggers and cyclists who invade a territory the dog tries to protect. If you see or hear a dog coming, quickly assess the situation: Is there another route you can take? Does the dog look sick or crazed? Is it simply defending its territory? Then, if you are on foot, keep facing the dog and begin jogging backward in any direction away from its territory. If you are on a bike, keep pedaling away from the dog's territory, using only one foot if necessary to protect yourself. In either case, it is helpful to growl or yell a few times as you are moving off. These actions demonstrate retreat but keep up a bold front that is usually successful. Whatever you do, don't let the dog get its teeth into your arm or leg.

Insect Bites

If you are stung by a bee, hornet, or yellow jacket, and the stinger is left in the wound, gently pull it out. Then apply ice to keep swelling down and follow with calamine lotion or a spray or ointment containing a topical anesthetic. But if you have any trouble breathing, begin to wheeze, or swelling is marked, go straight to an emergency room. These are the first signs of an allergic reaction.

19 / The Dangers of Heat

Heat Stroke

MOST cases of heat stroke occur during July and August, when the dog star Sirius rises with the hot morning sun. For this reason, the ancients blamed such strokes on Sirius and we came to have the term "dog days" and the medical name "siriasis" for heat stroke.

Heat stroke is the second leading cause of death in high-school athletes, and it is almost always preventable.

These are the signs of heat stroke:

1/ Headache, nausea, dizziness, or, worse, confusion.

2/ Hot dry skin.

3/ Rectal temperature above 105°F (40.6°C).

While it rarely gets too cold to exercise outdoors, it can certainly get too hot. In temperatures above ninety degrees Fahrenheit with 90 percent humidity, strenuous training is not recommended. Exercising in such heat is risky, unless you are in excellent condition and have trained in heat and humidity for more than two weeks. It takes at least that amount of time for the body to become adjusted to heat, regardless of one's overall condition.

The major causes of heat stroke are:

1/ Lack of training for more than two weeks in high heat and humidity.

2/ Being out of shape.

3/ Obesity.

4/ Drugs, principally amphetamines (uppers), tranquilizers, blood pressure medicines, anti-seizure medicines, and, especially, diuretics.

5/ Fear of admitting dizziness, nausea, headache, or cramps. This happens particularly in athletes who keep on training, in spite of the early symptoms of heat stroke. The risk of such exertion is death, especially if the individual doesn't stop, cool off, and drink a sufficient amount of water. If a coach will not permit an athlete to stop, it could be the equivalent of a death sentence.

6/ Plastic sweatsuits. People have died of heat stroke exercising in plastic suits at temperatures of eighty degrees Fahrenheit (26.6°C). Body temperature can rise at a rate of nine Fahrenheit degrees (five Celsius) per hour in a plastic suit, and the suit makes it impossible for the skin to perform its normal cooling function. Water, not fat, is lost by sweating, and the brain is being cooked and muscle is being destroyed under those conditions.

Prevention of Heat Stroke

To avoid heat stroke, pay attention to the following recommendations.

1/ Don't work out in the afternoon during the dog days of July and August, especially if the temperature is above 32 degrees Celsius (about 90°F) with 90 percent humidity.

2/ Drink lots of water, or, if you are coaching, provide plenty of fresh, cool water for your players.

3/ Salt tablets are good, but a lot of water and a little salt is better than a lot of salt and a little water. I emphasize this because the body conserves salt better than water. Also, salt usually gets overemphasized and probably isn't necessary after two weeks of training and heat.

4/ If it is hot and humid, do not wear football uniforms and helmets during the first two weeks of practice.

5/ Never wear a plastic suit if the temperature is above eighty degrees (26.6°C).

6/ If you become nauseated, start to vomit, feel dizzy, or develop muscle cramps, stop all activity, get in the shade to cool off, drink plenty of water, and splash yourself with water. Any of these symptoms will be aggravated by continued activity. If you are by yourself and fail to stop in time, you could die before you are found.

Emergency Treatment for Heat Stroke

1/ Get out of the sun and into the shade.

2/ Cool off. Hose down and drink water. Stand in front of a fan or air conditioner.

3/ If headache, dizziness, or confusion persists and your temperature is above 101 degrees (38.5°C) prompt hospital treatment is necessary.

The Importance of Sweat

Vigorous exercise will increase body temperature to a range of 38.5 to 40 degrees Celsius (101° to 104°F). This is desirable in cold weather, but makes it difficult or impossible to cool off when it is hot.

Sweat is the body's cooling mechanism, or radiator. It is not an indicator of how hard we work, but of how hot we become while working. The amount of sweat a person produces can vary tremendously, from as little as none to more than a gallon (about four liters) an hour. Theoretically, while sweating at maximum, a person can lose up to nine pounds (about four kilograms) an hour. Someone who is used to the heat and has built up a tolerance sweats more than a person who is not acclimated, because his or her cooling mechanism is working properly. But it takes at least two weeks to become used to hot weather, no matter what condition the body is in.

Another type of sweating can be caused by mental stress. This stress activates the sweat glands of the armpits and palms of the hand, which are not usually involved in heat control. These glands produce most, but obviously not all, of the sweat odor.

An athlete who loses up to a gallon of sweat an hour in the heat necessarily becomes very thirsty. That is why access to an unlimited amount of water is mandatory when it is hot. Water is not only the best replacement fluid for sweat, but the amount of water consumed should be equivalent to the amount of weight lost. Cool water is best because water that is ice cold sometimes feels unpleasant when gulped down, and it may cause an irregular heart beat in a few vulnerable people.

The athlete unused to heat will lose large amounts of salt at first, but the loss will decrease to a minimum as the body adjusts to hot weather. Salt tablets are excellent for an unacclimatized person who needs to replace lost salt, but regular tomato juice or a tomato juice cocktail are also good for this purpose. Fruit juices and the "ades" also have varying concentrations of salt and calories, but sodas are carbonated, which causes gas. That problem can be eliminated by shaking an opened can or bottle of soda until the bubbles have been released.

Iron is the third important substance that is lost in sweat. This loss of iron is usually negligible, but it can be a problem if it occurs for lengthy periods of time. (Swimmers sweat, but may not realize it in the water.) Iron loss can also be a problem in female athletes because they lose iron in their menstrual fluids as well as in sweat. This deficiency can lead to anemia and fatigue.

Index

Numbers in *italics* indicate illustrations.